NO LONGER PROPERTY OF
SEATTLE PUBLIC LIBRARY

D0981922

Doing Psychoanalysis in Tehran

Doing Psychoanalysis *in* Tehran

Gohar Homayounpour

foreword by Abbas Kiarostami

The MIT Press   Cambridge, Massachusetts   London, England

© 2012 Massachusetts Institute of Technology

All rights reserved. No part of this book may be reproduced in any form by any electronic or mechanical means (including photocopying, recording, or information storage and retrieval) without permission in writing from the publisher.

MIT Press books may be purchased at special quantity discounts for business or sales promotional use. For information, please email special_sales@mitpress.mit.edu or write to Special Sales Department, The MIT Press, 55 Hayward Street, Cambridge, MA 02142.

This book was set in Garamond Premier Pro by The MIT Press. Printed and bound in the United States of America.

Library of Congress Cataloging-in-Publication Data

Homayounpour, Gohar, 1977–
    Doing psychoanalysis in Tehran / Gohar Homayounpour ; foreword by
    Abbas Kiarostami.
    p. ; cm.
    ISBN 978-0-262-01792-3 (hardcover : alk. paper)
    1. Title.
    [DNLM: 1. Psychotherapy—Iran. 2. Cultural Characteristics—Iran.
    3. Psychoanalysis—methods—Iran. WM 420]

616.89'140095525—dc23

                                                                    2012005688

10 9 8 7 6 5 4 3 2 1

To Darya and Yassamine, for being who they are

Contents

Foreword

The first thing that impressed me as I began to read this book was how the world that Gohar Homayounpour explores through the psychoanalytic lens closely resembles what I see through the lens of my camera. I caught myself smiling and then realized that I was thinking about an old Iranian saying: "Jana sokhan az zabane ma migooi." "Dear, you speak from my heart!"

The truth is that neither of us considers our world merely a personal space where the slightest discord might bring discontent. Neither is this world of ours a public court of law where we sit in judgment of others' private tragedies; we are only observing the illusive world of everyday life through multiple lenses, hoping to bring some sense to it through reflection and analysis. We try our best not to be provincial observers. Our world is not limited to our neighborhood, our city, or even our motherland. "Pain is pain everywhere," as Gohar Homayounpour says about the experience of doing psychoanalysis in Tehran and in the United States. For years I have been trying to convey the same message. My films attempt to express the human condition rather than the specific conditions or masks that localize this or the other group or person.

I know from experience how hard it is to explore this existential condition without falling into the trap of clichés, of the status quo, and of all that we take as given and as intransigently real. It is not an easy task for anyone, and I am sure that it has not been easy for Gohar Homayounpour to break away from clichés, to leave the sanctuary of stereotypes, and give up the pleasure of adhering to simpleminded images of the other. Of course, these days, there is a good market for films and books that portray Iran and Iranians in stereotypical terms. Homayounpour would have easily gained popularity by painting an evocative and passionate *orientalist* caricature of Iranians that would reinforce people's prejudices. She could have even gotten her work on the bestseller list. Resisting this temptation is undeniably a sign of nobility, dignity, sincerity, and, last but not least, evidence of an independent and original mind. It was this aspect of the writer that encouraged me to write this foreword; the brave sincerity, the original writing style, and the level of discourse that is indeed worthy of praise and admiration.

It was particularly fascinating to me—as I'm sure it will be to other readers—to experience her world through her words, and her complicated psychoanalytic encounters through her sophisticated and unassuming narration. What is apparently the account of her own story involving her relationship with her patients in Tehran put me in touch with my own personal story involving my relationships.

At this point, let me assure you in no uncertain terms that I would not recommend this book to those who are still searching for the "touristic attractions" of my country. Luckily for those people, the production of that kind of literature, films, paintings, and photography is prospering these days! However, Homayounpour's book is an extraordinary work that is recommended for those who consider human pain and suffering as an existential phenomenon. Pain is beyond doubt pain everywhere; I have never heard of an Eastern or

Western cancer or of a radiography that would show the nationality, religion, language, or culture of the patient. This book is a radiographic picture of the human condition in Iran, not a touristic photograph of Iranians.

Gohar Homayounpour did not choose the easy way out, and remained faithful to the title of the book: *Doing Psychoanalysis in Tehran*. This is in fact the account of the experience of a psychoanalyst working in today's Tehran, an account that continues to grow on you, gets you to know her as an analyst, surprises you, and makes you question your own presuppositions. Imagine how I was pleasantly surprised when I read that the Iranian women in the book do not narrate the injustices and the oppression that they face in our society today, but talk about the internal paradoxes, conflicts, and dualities they experience while coming face to face with their womanhood—just like any other women in the world.

I definitely consider Gohar Homayounpour's achievement an uncommon one. In the format of a biographical novel, and using psychoanalytic free association, she opens up windows and sheds light onto the darkness of the human soul. She pursues the task elegantly recommended by

Freud: "Now that it is impossible to see clearly, let us try to shed light upon darkness."

For all these reasons, I would like to congratulate Dr. Homayounpour for the freshness and authenticity of her discourse, and welcome her to my world.

Abbas Kiarostami
Tehran, summer 2011

Preface

Is Psychoanalysis Possible in the Islamic Republic of Iran?

As the title *Doing Psychoanalysis in Tehran* implies, what you are about to encounter is an attempt to write in the format of a psychoanalytic session; an "ideal" psychoanalytic session where both analytic subjects, analyst and analysand, have the courage to face the chaos of their unconscious, to come face to face with the stranger within themselves, and to learn to bear the anxiety of participating in the unknown.

The reader will not find chapters, footnotes, or exact referencing. I have attempted to avoid the defenses provided by classification and labeling. Julia Kristeva recounts that, having written many scientific papers and books on different topics, she has come to the conclusion over the years that at some level they perform a defensive function. One can authentically face oneself only in the highly intimate process of writing a novel.

In this process one finds oneself far away from the safety provided by a specific structure, the comfort of the certainties associated with categorizing, and the inevitable anxiety that follows in the absence of any frame of reference.

Writing a paper for a scientific journal (without in any way intending to detract from the necessity of such endeavors) is like a patient coming into a session and verbalizing that he has thought about what to say, how to say, and in what order to say the things that must be communicated to the analyst. It is as though he still has the illusion that when using the imperfect tool of language there is such a thing as the possibility of exact communication, and he doesn't realize that all we are capable of doing is miscommunicating. It is as though he uses the defense of illusory precision to deal with the anxiety of being on the analytic couch.

In a good-enough analytic environment, the analysand slowly becomes brave enough to let go of his symbolic pieces of paper and specific categories, and his desire to know often prevails over the comfort of staying away from the things that his unconscious already knows.

Certainly, there always remains the question of how free one's free associations actually are. This I will try to address in the following pages, in which I have attempted to free-associate in Tehran. These pages are nothing but my fantasies and my fantasies alone (not that anyone can get away from doing anything else), where I once again indulge in the challenge of coming face to face with my own unconscious.

In a sense, this is solely a note to myself.

I have been practicing psychoanalysis in Tehran for the last five years. Meanwhile, I have written a number of papers about my experience as a psychoanalyst in Iran, and presented them at international conferences. I have been interviewed by a number of Western radio stations and magazines on this topic, and written the book you are reading. My experience of speaking in different venues about doing psychoanalysis in Iran has been interesting. The audience's reaction to my account has been quite curious. I would characterize this reaction as a "fascinated rejection," to borrow Julia Kristeva's expression.

The topic of doing psychoanalysis in Iran conjures up some fascinating fantasies from the start; the listener usually anticipates some juicy, exotic stories. Yet this fascination is accompanied by a rejection, suggesting the impossibility of doing psychoanalysis in Iran. I feel that

I have almost caused disappointment by presenting case materials that are similar to those of patients in Boston or New York.

These reactions could also be characterized as a form of "orientalism," to borrow Edward Said's term. The exotic (or oriental) Other is fascinating for the Westerner, but the gaze is one that makes the Other inferior; it is not the same kind of exoticness that is generally attributed to the French.

However, without going into the details of Said's theoretical position, I would like to add the responsibility of the "Orientals" themselves in creating orientalism, according to his theory. We have to stop blaming the West for our condition, for our destiny.

In fact, if you are reading this book in order to satisfy your orientalist curiosities, I have to warn you: it will be a disappointing experience.

I know it is popular to eroticize the chador, to use exotic titles such as *Lipstick Jihad*, talk about how Iranian men beat their wives, or eroticize Iranian calligraphy, such as *aleph, be, ce,* using exotic names like *Shehrazad, Syavash, Mahmoud Hussein*. I am not blaming this phenomenon on the "Other," we do it to ourselves. We are attached to our oriental reflection in the eyes of the Other.

A French friend recently reminded me that "the French are also eroticized in various ways." But I believe there is a difference between being eroticized for crème brûlée and being eroticized through the chador. The former is not a manifestation of the master-slave mentality; the French are eroticized for their superiority, while the Orientals are desirable for their inferior delights.

I am not playing the blame game; we do it to ourselves, for there are so many neurotic gains to be had from the process.

Change starts within ourselves. We have to give up the pleasures of being looked upon as erotic, exotic, and strange. We have to come face to face with our inevitable ordinariness.

Slavoj Žižek, in a recent interview, said that what he admires about Abbas Kiarostami movies is that one does not get any images of daily life in Iran; that they represent universal conflicts. I come from the same school of thought.

Recently I sent a paper, "The Couch and the Chador," to a prominent Lacanian psychoanalyst for her comments. She wrote back:

To me, here, you offer . . . the sociological lessons to be drawn from the impossibility of practicing psychoanalysis in Iran—It is a beautiful investigation of the Iranian making of the self. Where the Oedipal complex is played out according to very different parameters than in the West . . . everything is upside down. The Symbolic Order—or rather what replaces it, a rigid structure reminiscent of mechanical solidarity superimposed upon the greatest civilization of all time, which went under repression along with their desirous men—is the backdrop for the child of what regulates the all-powerful desire of the mother . . . this is why the postmodern definitions of femininity and body feel to me problematic, since there is no direct indictment of the patriarchal order, since there is none in the Western sense of the term. Anyways, psychoanalysis can't really work *in Iran*, as it is after all a purely Western practice.

According to this analyst, psychoanalysis is impossible in Iran—not only because it is a Western practice, but also because Iranians operate within a different symbolic order. In Iran the symbolic order is upside down: there is no entry into the Oedipus complex for the child, suggesting that the Iranian national psyche is psychotic.

Another psychoanalyst at a recent conference in Boston responded to a different paper of mine with "but I do not think that Iranians can free-associate!" I responded by saying that in my opinion they do nothing but, and that is their problem.

I also sent an early draft of my book to a very famous journalist who had been many times to Tehran, so I knew that she was fascinated by Iran.

This is what she wrote back to me:

> I checked with a friend who runs a publishing company, and he suggested that you pick the most provocative couple of chapters, chapters that would appeal to an American public, and email them to him. (It should not be psychoanalytic material that a psychoanalyst could write in Manhattan: it should be juicy.)
>
> I wonder how in the world a psychoanalyst can even function in Iran. I wonder if any ayatollahs have sought help.

Is Psychoanalysis Possible in the Islamic Republic of Iran?

You should give the chapters a zippier title. (*On the Couch in Iran*, for instance, is better: zippier!) I'm curious about how many patients you actually treat in Tehran. Are there any patients outside of Tehran? Do any prisoners get psych treatments?

Do you ever worry that Iranian officials might try to find out what your patients are telling you? Have any of your patients been political prisoners?

Are the patients more likely to have sexual or political problems? Or do these sometimes converge? [Apparently, according to this journalist, these are the only two kinds of problems an Iranian might have!]

How about you change your title to *Going Crazy in Tehran*?

This is what I mean by the "fascinated rejection." Iranians are "aliens," these very strange, exotic creatures. Who is this stranger? Why alien—and alien to whom?

According to Deleuze and Guattari, the impossibility of being "in your own home" provides us with an ontological misunderstanding: the tragedy of identity.

"Worrying strangeness" is a Freudian concept used by Kristeva as one explanation of this tragedy: "The fear of the Other and the worry of strangeness are both the result of the fear of the difference of the Other (stranger) within ourselves." We are scared of what we are and we are scared of our unleashed desires. Hence we transfer our fear to the Other, to the stranger, to the one who is not "us," and to the "difference." The Other is both the source of our anxiety, and the danger which threatens us.

The fear that we experience, the strangeness, is more of an internal phenomenon than an external one. The "worrying strangeness" can never compete with the fear and the anxiety of facing our unconscious, our femininity, or with the fear of facing death. The worrying strangeness is closely related to the childish fear of the Other: the Other in the form of death, the Other in the form of woman, and the Other in the form of our own uncontrollable drives . . . in short, the fear of the Other as the stranger within ourselves.

The fight we put up against this is the same fight we put up against our own unconscious, and the only possible Derridean hospitality we could offer would be to accept and welcome these strangers into the fearful territory in which we (the stranger and the self) are both living!

According to Kristeva, living with the Other is living with this question: "Am I the Other?"

Or, as the French poet Rimbaud puts it: "I is an other."

Kristeva wonders why we call foreigners "aliens," alien being anything entirely Other to the status quo. But an "alien" is also the scary foreign body in the eponymous movie which prevented us from sleeping for such a long time. What if Kristeva is right, and the hidden face of our identity is the alien who lives within us? Facing the Other thus becomes comparable to facing the "strange identity," the "troublesome otherness," that Freud introduced to us when he theorized the existence of the unconscious. I cannot deal with you, "the alien," just as I cannot deal with the alien inside me. There is something in you that disturbs the unconscious alien within myself.

I was interviewed for the Italian psychoanalytic journal *Psyche*, and although in this case the interviewer was a lot more in touch with the alien within herself, and treated psychoanalysis in Iran with a much more open mind than the other examples I have given, there were still certain questions she asked, and a certain manner in which she asked them, that reinforce the point we have been discussing thus far.

She asked:

There are various psychoanalytical theories on trauma and on how to treat traumatized patients. They all agree on the fact that past and present traumatic experiences can be worked through in the transference and the analytical relationship. If this is true, and I hope it is, then psychoanalytic treatment can reduce the suffering arising from traumatic experiences linked to restrictive and destructive familiar and social situations. It is very important to distinguish the cultural from the political in Iran, which does not seem to be the same as in the West, and favor the passage from being subject to one's own story to being the subject of it, which is to say an active agent of one's own story and one's own destiny, in a way relatively independent from the environmental, social, and cultural context. Could you comment on this?

I answered: "Of course, if the subject has the desire to work through his or her traumas, this desire should always prevail over the environmental, social, and cultural contingencies. However, we should not forget that subject itself is a cultural artifact along with the mode of its liberation, i.e. psychoanalysis. To transcend the symbolic order in order to become one's own agent or an autonomous ego is an intriguing fantasy, which should operate in Lacan's imaginary register."

In your view, has the interest in and curiosity about psychoanalysis as a means of treating mental problems, and also its introduction to Iran, resembled the transplantation of a foreign body by professionals or intellectuals who have been educated abroad? Or, conversely, has it found a fertile ground for its development within the cultural and artistic (poetry, miniatures, carpets) traditions and the spiritual strength which are, according to the famous Iranian poet Ferdousi, the expressive means through which Iran has always communicated with the outside world?

I answered: "It is both; psychoanalysis was transplanted here from the West, but in quite a special manner. The seeds of this Western discovery found a very fertile ground within the culture of Iranian thought. Ferdousi, to whom you referred, can be considered our Sophocles. In him we see the significance of storytelling, dialog, and interpersonal relationships ingrained within the Iranian historical tradition.

"So we brought the seed of psychoanalysis from the West, but in Iran this seed found itself germinating in and nurtured by various artistic expressions such the ones you have mentioned. For example, every carpet has a story to tell through its unique and specific design, and has been made with the intention of communicating with a specific Other. Iranian culture revolves around stories. People here are very much into talking, talking, and talking; and so the talking cure has found itself taken to the heart of the Iranian national character."

I am not ignoring the importance of cultural difference, yet neither can we ignore the fact that human beings are a lot more similar than they are different, that pain is pain and whenever we feel differently, we must look for the stranger within. That is the only place we will find an alien, a stranger.

I do not need any of the theories outlined above to understand the possibility of doing psychoanalysis in Iran. I am reminded by my patients during every minute of their 50-minute-long analytic sessions, every single day, that we are doing psychoanalysis.

What I would like to do is to report on some of these experiences, these co-constructed fantasies of this particular analyst and her patients after her return home to Iran.

Upon Arriving
in Tehran

She isn't the first patient I have seen in Tehran. Last summer, while vacationing in Iran, I worked with a few patients, and it is certainly not the first time that I find myself waiting for a new one. As it is, I cannot understand where the anguish, the nervousness, and the lack of confidence come from. Does it all have to do with the referral source, an ego ideal of mine? What if I cannot keep the patient? What if she thinks I am too young? What if I cannot find the right words in Farsi—what if I do not end up being the brilliant psychoanalyst I have convinced my ego ideal I have become?

But maybe it has to do with what I have heard about Ms. N. I have heard about *her* brilliance, her straightforwardness. I have also been told that while asking for a referral she questioned my doctorate in psychoanalysis.

But maybe it has to do with being in a new environment, and to some extent having become free of some imaginary master-signifiers. I have no one to answer to. I can work exactly the way I want, the way I believe. I am free. (At least it seemed easier at the time to have the illusion of freedom. Four years later, I must say that this illusion has been completely destroyed.) So what is wrong? What is so very wrong? Do we need master-signifiers? What will I do with this freedom, and why is it so terrifying?

I think, now, that I found myself scared and nervous, for who was I if I was not the rebellious psychoanalyst fighting for subjectivity? Now I had been given the subjectivity I had wanted in the form of a doctorate and certification as an analyst, but my titles brought a great deal more upon me than the usual authority accompanied by such degrees.

I have moved to Tehran with my degree in my ego ideal's suitcase, and now I have an open field, lots of patients, and no one to answer to. I do not need to play any political games, none whatsoever, in Tehran. Ironically, this privilege has been given to me in a country that at this moment in history is one of the most politicized countries in the world. A country stigmatized by the world for its violations of human rights, its lack of democracy, its nuclear ambitions, and its lack of freedom of speech.

In Tehran, in one of the most controversial countries in the world, I have gotten closer to my rights as a psychoanalyst than I could have done elsewhere. Paradoxically, I have found my place, having been spared the usual politics that recent graduates of any psychoanalytic institute have to endure in the rest of the world.

And yet I find myself anguished . . .

The patient walks in; she is tall, well dressed, not beautiful, even though one cannot help noticing the remaining traces of what was once upon a time a striking woman. Right away I notice there is a certain air about her. She walks gracefully, firmly: confident, and yet vulnerable. I show her to my office, and my anguish is lifted as soon as I utter the words "What brings you here?" Ah, the magic of these words, these four words which are loaded for me; they immediately put me in the analytic position, they grant me confidence. They hold the many voices and ghosts of analysts past inside them; they are my analytic organ, as Julia Kristeva would say. But in the midst of feeling confident I am brought down once again, faced with my own castration, when I notice that she is sitting on my chair and I on the couch!

How did this happen? Yet I am betrayed by language and I say nothing.

She starts telling me: "You know, Dr. Homayounpour, when I heard about a fresh, young psychoanalyst coming to Tehran, I got your number and I came right away, for I need help, and I need you to help me. However, I do not want to talk about my emergency problem today. I want to ask you a few questions, but I hear that isn't kosher in psychoanalysis. Listen, I know Lacan and Freud very well, I was analyzed by a Jungian psychoanalyst years back. I am a famous painter. I lived in Paris for years and I hated every minute of it. I find French people rough. Eventually I fell into a depression seven years ago and it broke me inside." She starts crying and wonders: "How come you make me cry so easily, little girl?"

Having faced my silence to her question, she responds to her own question with two dreams. She tells me that her recurring dream consists of being told that she has to get all her stuff together because of some form of disaster. She has to pack, mostly her clothes, to join everybody else on an enormous ship that is leaving the city; and yet each time she is unable to fully dress herself. Anxiety takes over in every episode of the dream, leaving the dreamer unable to find the last article of clothing, such as a pair of shoes, her blouse, her jacket, etc., in order to be able to join the departing ship.

As I listen to Ms. N, I notice her hands, *her* professional organ as a painter. Her fingers are all deformed, her skin is dry and irritated. Both her arms have a strange twist to them, and I know right away that this is a severe case of arthritis.

I find myself drifting away from her into my own psychic stage. I wonder if this is a clue as to why I found myself on the couch earlier, when she cut off my analytic organ by situating herself on my chair.

Arthritis has shown her no mercy; it has slowly taken over her professional organs, and she is not capable of easily handing me the thing that has been so abruptly and severely taken away from her. That would just not be fair, it seems, in the psychic world of Ms. N.

She goes on: "The second dream I have is about my mother. You know, this dream often perplexes me, because in real life my mother was the typical Iranian mother, who would sacrifice everything for her children. Yet in the dream I am a little girl, trying to call upon her, trying to get her attention. I cry and shout and nothing works, for she is very beautifully dressed, dancing to superb music and pre-occupied with a great number of men. She does not even turn to look at me."

There is something about this dream that sends shivers down my spine; I desperately want to come up with some-thing to say to Ms. N, but the words do not make themselves available to me. I find myself hating her mother, thinking in silence: "I guess she was not so self-sacrificing after all, if the language of your unconscious is reminding you of not having been heard by her, and yet consciously you have managed to remember her as a saint, the image of a dream mother, whom every child desires." But it seems that Ms. N cannot flee from the horrifying images of a very different kind of mother. The mother who does not respond to you no matter how desperately you try to make her, the mother who refuses to put you under her gaze, the mother of every child's nightmare. It seems that Ms. N's days are accompa-nied by the mother of her dreams, while she cannot escape the mother of her nightmares at night.

The last dream brings with it a shift in the dynamic Ms. N and I share; she is the little girl now, and I have restored my analytic position, even though she is still sitting on my chair!

I ask her to elaborate on her dreams, and she says: "You know, most days I shout so much at people around me that I lose my voice, and that is not even what tortures me the most. The worst is the torment that accompanies me, joined by severe guilt after my hysterical episodes. Why do I shout so much? I want to shout now!" I right away think of her shouting in her dream to get her mother's attention, to have her notice her, hear her, look at her. I inquire if there is anything she is saying that I am not hearing right now? She starts to cry again.

I have an idea that my last intervention has brought us closer, and this idea is strengthened by what follows. Ms. N reports: "The only time I have ever been on an analytic couch was when I lived in Paris. I met a famous psycho-analyst in a café, we sent the usual signals men and women send each other and we ended up in his office, on his couch, making very passionate love."

She has a mischievous smile as she tells me about her escapade in Paris, to which I respond: "So, you have been very well analyzed."

This exchange feels very intimate. I had been afraid that things were moving too fast. Now I wonder: too fast for whom? Is my concern really for Ms. N, or are things moving too fast for me? Are the intimacy and the sexual tone of our last conversation making me, the analyst, feel uncomfortable?

As my mind is spinning, playing with these various ideas, she tells me that our time is up. This again feels like an attempt to challenge my analytic position, perhaps to show me who has control over these sessions. I try to take the analyst's chair back, so to speak, and bring up the issue of the fee. *I* have a mischievous smile now; there is nothing like bringing up the fee to clarify any misunderstandings about who is in charge, and who is going to be charged. My communication to her is: you may take my chair, you may be the one ending the session, but let me remind you who is going to pay whom. You are here to see me; you are here to get something from me that you believe I have, and for that you will have to pay me.

Freud understood the loaded symbolization of money when he wrote: "Money matters will be treated by cultured people in the same manner as sexual matters, with the same inconsistency, prudishness and hypocrisy."

While I am still very proud of the recent reclaiming of my chair (she is tough and does not give up the match easily), she throws me another ball and says: "Would you like cash? Many psychoanalysts have a fetish about good old hard cash."

I am not going to lose. I cannot afford to lose this game right now; I am too attached to my position as an analyst to let her win. I have lost too many of my imaginary positions recently. I am not going to give this one up without a fight.

As it is, I reply: "Pay me with whatever fetish *you* have." She smiles, a smile that in my opinion feels like a warning, foreshadowing our sessions to come, but a smile that also has some degree of satisfaction in it. I imagine that she feels I could be a worthy opponent.

As she gets up from *my* chair and heads for the door, she says: "Wipe your sweat away, you did well!" I can't believe it: "Wipe your sweat away, you did well!"

How I am reminded of Milan Kundera. How I abuse him, as a master (everyone knows that it is not only slaves who are abused by masters). I have internalized him as the novelist who mastered the *Art of the Novel*. I had a dream about him last night; I remember it in black and white (surely I have made it black and white because, as beautiful as colors can be, I cannot help but associate a certain kind of banality with them, and the director of my unconscious refuses to assign any form of banality to Kundera).

But what is wrong with banality? In my opinion, everything. I despise it in others, I am incapable of forgiving it in myself. Hell is not the Other, but banality. It is not the Marquis de Sade who should be burned, but banality.

In an interview about her novel *The Samurai*, Julia Kristeva wisely elaborates: "None of the characters in the Samurai could say that hell is other people, for hell is inside of us. Neither can they ask the question, 'Should we burn Sade?' for Sade is burning inside of us."

If we share, as I do, Kristeva's Freudian position, then we can infer this: is it not my very own banality, burning inside of me, that has paved the way for my deep rejection of banality? That being said, in my opinion banality remains the fundamental diagnostic criterion of the crisis within our era.

Let us go back to my dream, and Milan Kundera telling me: "I like what you are writing these days." When I get up I feel that I might as well have dreamt of an ice cream: that this, indeed, is the wish fulfillment of our dreams. The dream is also a reminder of my narcissism, with the language of my unconscious making the master novelist tell *me* how much he likes my writing.

What you do not yet know about my intimate love affair with Kundera is that it goes back to many years ago, to when I was eleven years old. That year I read *The Unbearable Lightness of Being* in Farsi. I read it word by word, at least five times, and had many parts memorized by heart.

One of the frequent limitations in the psychoanalytic study of literature is an emphasis on content at the expense of form. This tendency is often accompanied by a "pseudo-clinical" approach, which treats fictional characters as if they were flesh-and-blood human beings undergoing analysis. Naturally, treating characters as our patients allows us to stay in familiar territory and to avoid issues with which we may be less familiar, such as the unique structure and tradition of literature.

Although I find myself in agreement with Berman's general thesis, as outlined above, I cannot refrain from attempting the psychoanalysis of the characters in *The Unbearable*

Lightness of Being—characters who, over the years, have come to seem almost more like flesh and blood to me than many of the "real" people I have analyzed.

Borges's elegant turn of phrase elaborates my feelings:

A tiger comes to mind. The twilight here
Exalts the vast and busy Library
And seems to set the bookshelves back in gloom;
Innocent, ruthless, bloodstained, sleek
It wanders through its forest and its day
Printing a track along the muddy banks
Of sluggish streams whose names it does not know
(In its world there are no names or past
Or time to come, only the vivid now)
And makes its way across wild distances
Sniffing the braided labyrinth of smells
And in the wind picking the smell of dawn
And tantalizing scent of grazing deer;
Among the bamboo's slanting stripes I glimpse
The tiger's stripes and sense the bony frame
Under the splendid, quivering cover of skin.
Curving oceans and the planet's wastes keep us

Apart in vain; from here in a house far off
In South America I dream of you,
Track you, O tiger of the Ganges' banks.

It strikes me now as evening fills my soul
That the tiger addressed in my poem
Is a shadowy beast, a tiger of symbols
And scraps picked up at random out of books,
A string of labored tropes that have no life,
And not the fated tiger, the deadly jewel
That under sun or stars or changing moon
Goes on in Bengal or Sumatra fulfilling
Its rounds of love and indolence and death.
To the tiger of symbols I hold opposed
The one that's real, the one whose blood runs hot
As it cuts down a herd of buffaloes,
And that today, this August third, nineteen
Fifty-nine, throws its shadow on the grass;
But by the act of giving it a name,
By trying to fix the limits of its world,
It becomes a fiction not a living beast,
Not a tiger out roaming the wilds of earth.

Upon Arriving in Tehran

We'll hunt for a third tiger now, but like
The others this one too will be a form
Of what I dream, a structure of words, and not
The flesh and one tiger that beyond all myths
Paces the earth. I know these things quite well,
Yet nonetheless some force keeps driving me
In this vague, unreasonable, and ancient quest,
And I go on pursuing through the hours
Another tiger, the beast not found in verse.

While we should be wary of sacrificing form for content, can we really find a more genuine tiger than the one described in Borges's verse? Is a real flesh-and-blood tiger really any more vivid, striking, exciting, terrifying, and authentic than the one made out of Borges's imagination?

To those who say that characters in a novel do not have their own unconscious, but are only fragments of the unconscious of their author, I say: "I know these things quite well, and yet nonetheless some force keeps driving me in this vague, unreasonable, and ancient quest, and I go on pursuing through the hours another tiger, the beast not found in verse."

Kundera in general and *The Unbearable Lightness of Being* in particular are, for me, the specific essence of what literature is about. No contemporary author has mastered *The Art of the Novel* as the writer of the work has himself.

Freud's long essay on the psychoanalysis of the German novelist Wilhelm Jensen's story "Gradiva" infuriated the writer, who did not want the characters he had created to be exposed or psychopathologized. I fear that Kundera would share Jensen's feelings, so it is with sincere apologies to the author of *The Unbearable Lightness of Being* that I start the psychoanalysis of its characters. These are characters who have over the years become my own versions of themselves within the theater of my mind. Since it is only possible for me to analyze my own versions; since within whatever we write it is only possible to reveal parts of our own unconscious and no more; since the author is dead, and long live the text; since it is only these various and limited levels of construction and interpretation that are possible, I plead for my apology to be accepted.

As I was saying, when I first read Kundera I was very young, and I remember being overwhelmed with such joyful sensations; I like to believe it was the same sort of joyfulness Nabokov experienced while hunting for butterflies.

I was certainly shaken by the language of the book; I began to love the characters. As I wondered about their choices, I would find myself in conversations with them. Sabina and her hats aroused my curiosity, but it was Tereza's fierce loyalty and the image of her two big suitcases that has never escaped me. Meanwhile Tomas did to my young heart what he managed to do to all women. I fell in love with him.

Franz, oh Franz. How I felt sorry for him. Today I am aware of having assigned to Franz one of the lowest emotions one can have for another person: to feel pity for him. Yet it was Karenin who brought tears to my eyes—never because I felt sorry for him, but because Karenin represented the antithesis of banality, the real antikitsch in my opinion. As it was, I cried and cried in the name of Karenin.

The Unbearable Lightness of Being was translated into Farsi in the year 1986. At that time Milan Kundera and the translator were both unknown to the Iranian public, and yet when *Bare Hasti* hit the bookstores, it was received with such enthusiasm that it shocked everyone involved.

Today *Bare Hasti* has been republished for the twentieth time; this is a record-breaking statistic in Iran. Over the years, the title of the book, and references to it, have become part of the intellectual discourse of the Iranian public. *The Unbearable Lightness of Being* has certainly assumed its weight in Iran.

The book starts with the philosophical struggle of lightness versus heaviness. Kundera wonders whether we could find meaning in life, if there is no possibility of Nietzsche's concept of eternal return. Since we all live life only once, and "the dress rehearsal for life is life itself," we are continuously faced with the meaninglessness of our lives. The shaky existence of meaning is the key question, and the opposition of lightness and heaviness the key dichotomy, of *The Unbearable Lightness of Being*. From a psychoanalytic perspective, this is the duality of life and death; lightness versus heaviness; Eros and Thanatos; this is, precisely, one of the chief struggles of the human condition.

Throughout *The Unbearable Lightness of Being*, Kundera familiarizes us with the way each of the characters in the book attempts to find their own balance between lightness and heaviness. He tells us about how these characters struggle in vain to obtain a state that is not totally unbearable.

The main protagonist, Tomas, a bright, handsome, and intellectual surgeon in Prague, is a womanizer on the surface, yet it is his curiosity, his desire to know, that takes him on many amorous adventures throughout the book. This, for Kundera, is precisely what differentiates the erotic from the sexual: a distinction which, he later claimed, was totally misunderstood by the American crew who produced the movie version of the work.

This important theme is brought up time after time in various contexts across the book. It seems that what distinguishes the erotic from the sexual has a direct relation to the object. In a sense, in the sexual our libido is pleasure-seeking, while in the erotic it seeks objects. And so in erotic relations we find a less narcissistic subject, with more awareness of the other, as opposed to pure sexuality, where the individual is absolutely unaware of the object.

Although Tomas makes a point of keeping a clear line between sex and love, he seems to be adept only at having erotic relationships. He keeps his eyes open at all times while making love to a woman, in order to be able to watch all the specificity of his lover's way of being. Every object he chooses has a clear relationship to something that is triggered within his unconscious fantasy. In short, Tomas's amorous adventures have an epistemological basis; he is in search of the ontology of every single woman he chooses.

Tomas's behavior comes at the high price of continuous torture for his wife Tereza, a simple waitress from the countryside who loves him with fierce devotion and loyalty. In Tereza, one finds heaviness, very well symbolized by the image of her two big, heavy suitcases. Tereza, in some parts of the book, is a woman who has successfully submitted to her castration: the essence of what moves the individual from neurotic misery to common unhappiness, as Freud tells us. Accepting one's castration is what is considered the cure for neurotics in psychoanalysis, but it seems that Tereza, like a specific group of our neurotic women patients, has confused submitting to one's castration with submission to the other—in her case to Tomas, her husband.

Upon applying for a photography job, Tereza is asked to take pictures of cactuses as a starting point. To this she replies that since she does not find cactuses interesting, and her husband can financially support her, she does not see any purpose in taking pictures of cactuses. The conversation goes as follows:

Upon Arriving in Tehran

The woman said, "But will you be fulfilled sitting at home?"

Tereza said, "More fulfilled than taking pictures of cactuses."

The woman said, "Even if you take pictures of cactuses, you're leading *your* life. If you only live for your husband, you have no life of your own."

All of a sudden Tereza felt annoyed: "My husband is my life, not cactuses."

The woman photographer responded in kind: "You mean you think of yourself as happy?"

Tereza, still annoyed, said, "Of course I am happy!"

The woman said, "The only kind of woman who can say that is very . . ." She stopped short.

Tereza finished it for her ". . . limited. That's what you mean, isn't it?"

The woman regained control of herself and said, "Not limited. Anachronistic."

"You're right," said Tereza wistfully. "That's just what my husband says about me."

In this passage we observe a Tereza who has successfully submitted to the reality of her castration, very well elaborated in her lack of desire for the phallus, itself symbolized by the phallic cactuses. She knows she does not possess a cactus and she is OK with that; this enables her to avoid being challenged or upset when she is called passé or old-fashioned. On the contrary, she says: "That is just what my husband says about me."

It is crystallized in the above passage that submitting to one's castration is in fact a matter of taking the route toward one's real desires, and not merely submitting to the Other. If she does not find cactuses interesting, she gladly lets her husband support her, and allows herself to pursue her real desires.

At other times Tereza seems to be caught in the repetitiveness of a sadomasochistic dynamic. She seems to enjoy the suffering that being with Tomas inevitably entails; she seems to partly enjoy her role as the victim of his actions. She gets to be a moralist. It is only because he is the one who cheats that she comes to identify herself as the one who does not. If we were to imagine Tereza in a love affair with Franz, who is also righteous, she would become absolutely meaningless.

And so, at one point in the novel when we see Tereza trying to cheat on Tomas with another man, she knows this is precisely the thing which might endanger the continued existence of their relationship. For their love has always been built upon her loyalty, not his; without her loyalty their relationship would fall apart.

Could Tereza's attachment to a sadomasochistic dynamic have to do with her relationship with her mother, which bordered on hate? Could it be that she is repeating the victimhood she has always felt in regard to her mother? The mother had always found her daughter the chief reason for all her disappointments in life, since it was after getting pregnant with Tereza that she felt doomed to stay in an unhappy marriage.

Then there is Sabina, whose life is described as a series of betrayals: "Betrayal means breaking ranks and going off into the unknown. Sabina knew of nothing more magnificent. . . ." Sabina's love affair with Tomas is based on their mutual lightness, although they are both intensely drawn to heaviness.

Sabina is the phallic woman, who, unlike Tereza, finds nothing more horrifying than to face her castration, which is very well symbolized by her hat. The hat has been passed on to her by the men of her family, the men who attempted to repress her desires, who tried to limit her possibilities. Sabina, it seems, has made an unconscious pact with herself never to let them win, thus their hat becomes a toy for her erotic games. It is as though she has become the master of the hat, as opposed to becoming its slave, the destiny that she fears the men of her ancestry have envisioned for her.

She refuses to submit to her castration, to stay in one place, to love, to become dependent, to see her impotence and lack of control; in short, to witness her Lacanian lack.

In a sense, submitting to one's castration in Kunderan terms could be elaborated like this: that it is the submission to the unbearable nature of being. No matter what combination of lightness or heaviness one finds, the human condition is unbearable, and there is nothing we can do about it but submit to it; as is well shown in the various characters of the novel. Of all these characters, Sabina is the one furthest away from accepting her castration.

Tomas seems to get stuck between lightness and heaviness in his various attempts to master his Freudian Oedipus complex; he only manages to situate himself within triangular relationships. He has abandoned his son, and overcompensates for this in his relationship with Tereza. He loves her the way one loves a child. In her, he has managed a compromise formation: to find a child he can take care of in the place of the son he has abandoned. But this child is a daughter who loves and admires him, as opposed to a son who will eventually become a budding Oedipus himself.

On various occasions, Tomas makes reference to the moment when Tereza arrived on his doorstep, saying that he felt as if she was delivered in a basket. Is this not a reference to the historically famous son abandoned in a basket? He cannot send her away when she shows up unannounced, her life in her two big suitcases, begging him to, in a sense, adopt her. To take her away from her village, from her bartending job, and from her lightlessness. She needs him to achieve her own balance of lightness versus heaviness.

Tomas writes an article, condemning communist leaders' claim that they "did not know" atrocious crimes were happening at the time, that they only adhered to the communist ideology, as though if they did not know, they should be redeemed. Tomas compares them to Oedipus, and claims that Oedipus supposedly and consciously did not know what he had done; yet he gouged out his eyes once he realized, in order to punish himself.

From a psychoanalytic perspective we can read that Tomas is himself the Oedipus of his article, guilt-ridden by crimes he has unconsciously committed, and feels that the only way of redeeming himself is by receiving punishment. Tomas's unconscious need for punishment becomes clear throughout the book.

Tomas is unable to stop his amorous adventures, yet when Tereza suffers from various nightmares night after night due to his infidelity, we hear him say that he would rather watch his whole country burn down than hear her suffering as a result of a single nightmare.

The passage below elegantly elaborates on how Tomas loves Tereza:

> He suddenly recalled the famous myth from Plato's Symposium: People were hermaphrodites until God split them in two, and now all the halves wander the world over seeking one another. Love is the longing for the half of ourselves we have lost.
>
> Let us suppose that such is the case that somewhere in the world each of us has a partner who once formed part of our body. Tomas's other part is the young woman

he dreamed about. The trouble is, man does not find the other part of himself. Instead, he is sent Tereza in a bulrush basket. But what happens if he nevertheless later meets the one who was meant for him, the other part of himself? Whom is he to prefer? The woman from the bulrush basket or the one from Plato's myth?

He tries to picture himself living in an ideal world with the young woman from the dream. He sees Tereza walking past the open windows of their ideal house. She is alone and stops to look in at him with an infinitely sad expression in her eyes. He cannot withstand her glance. Again, he feels her pain in his own heart. Again, he falls prey to compassion and sinks deep into her soul. He leaps out of the window, but she tells him bitterly to stay where he feels happy, making those abrupt, angular movements that so annoyed and displeased him. He grabs her nervous hands and presses them between his own to calm them. And he knows that time and again he will abandon the house of his happiness, time and again abandon his paradise and the woman from his dream and betray the "Es muss sein!" of his love to go off with Tereza, the woman born of six laughable fortuities.

Lacan argues that it is impossible to say anything meaningful about love—indeed, for him, the moment one starts to speak about love, one descends into the imaginary. Paradoxically, he dedicates a great deal of time to love, and at the end of it all he claims that "the only thing that we do in the analytic discourse is speak about love." Kundera is, in the widest sense of the word, also merely speaking about love in *The Unbearable Lightness of Being*.

And nowhere is the novel more about love than when it comes to Karenin, Tomas and Tereza's dog. In the chapter entitled "Karenin's Smile," when they find out that their beloved dog has cancer, the reader moves from page to page with Tereza and Tomas, experiencing their heartbreaking grief until the end, when Tomas performs euthanasia on Karenin and they bury him. Nowhere in the entire novel are we left with the same unshakable sense of the unbearable lightness of being as when Karenin is brought to his death at the hands of his loved ones, for as Kundera tells us:

Dogs do not have many advantages over people, but one of them is extremely important: euthanasia is not forbidden by law in their case; animals have the right to a merciful death.

Stefano Bolognini, an Italian psychoanalyst, has a paper on the relationship between man and his dog, entitled "If Dogs Don't Go to Paradise, I Want to Go Where They Go." I believe that Kundera, like Bolognini, has intuitively understood what it really means to have had a dog and to have lost one. As such, Kundera rejects Descartes and adheres to Nietzsche, who holds the neck of a horse that has just been whipped and bursts into tears, apologizing on behalf of humanity. This is the Kundera we hear in the chapter on Karenin's smile, a Kundera who says:

> True human goodness, in all its purity and freedom, can come to the fore only when its recipient has no power. Mankind's true moral test, its fundamental test (which lies deeply buried from view), consists of its attitude towards those who are at its mercy: animals. And in this respect mankind has suffered a fundamental debacle, a debacle so fundamental that all others stem from it.

Karenin also performs as the obvious third within Tomas and Tereza's relationship; as the child they never had, he becomes the balancing element of lightness versus heaviness within it. Without him they cannot exist, so shortly after Karenin's death the unbearable lightness of being becomes too unbearable for Tomas and Tereza, and they also are killed in a car accident.

In Karenin we are given a model of loving; a model of what it means symbolically, in fact, to submit to one's castration.

It is completely selfless love: Tereza did not want anything of Karenin; she did not ever ask him to love her back. Nor has she ever asked herself the questions that plague human couples: Does he love me? Does he love anybody more than me? Does he love me more than I love him? Perhaps all the questions we ask of love, to measure, test, probe, and save it, have the additional effect of cutting it short. Perhaps the reason we are unable to love is that we yearn to be loved, that is, we demand something (love) from our partner instead of delivering ourselves to him demand-free and asking for nothing but his company.

Why did *The Unbearable Lightness of Being* enjoy such popularity everywhere, and especially in Iran?

Besides the fact that all the different characters provide various modes of identification for the reader, the numerous layers of the dilemmas of the human condition that Kundera provides, the genuine mastery of the art of the novel, and so on—besides all this, I believe, we love to read Kundera because his discourse is a lover's discourse, and solely a lover's discourse, and that intrigues us, challenges us, terrifies us. We might hate it, we might love it, but we cannot ignore it, and it is precisely the same with the psychoanalytic discourse.

At the end of *The Unbearable Lightness of Being*, everyone except Sabina dies. Meanwhile she, in America, is experiencing a sort of psychic death, and that existential human crisis, our inevitable death, is precisely why we are doomed to encounter the unbearable lightness of being. Nonetheless many of us choose life, for there is always the possibility of Karenin's smile.

All of the above analysis of *The Unbearable Lightness of Being* taken into account, what I remember the most is reading the last few pages of the book compulsively, over and over again. Each time, in my childhood fairytale fantasy, I hoped the ending would be different: that Tereza and Tomas would live happily ever after, with Karenin in their arms.

In the name of full exposure (if such a thing is possible), I have to say that my love relationship with Kundera also began because of the Farsi translator. My relationship with the translator of *The Unbearable Lightness of Being* goes even further back than my relationship with Kundera.

I had a very ambivalent relationship with the translator; a very difficult one, to say the least. I would find myself furious at him most of the time, and even more furious the rest of the time. So how come I had fallen in love with the book he had just translated, carrying it with me everywhere I went, underlining various parts in different colors? I had become a Kundera fan with all the intensity and passion available to the immature heart of an eleven-year-old girl. I would desperately try to come up with intelligent questions for the translator, only to hear him say: "My dear naïve daughter, you are too young to understand."

Did Kundera stand in my dream for my father? Am I still using Kundera the way I used him many years back, as a secret, indirect way of connecting to my father, of transmitting to him all the *unbearable* love I was unconsciously feeling for him? You see, I do abuse Kundera and, my memory informs me, I have done for many years.

Sometime in those same distant years, after he had translated *The Unbearable Lightness of Being*, my father took a trip to Paris, and at some point on the airplane from Tehran to Paris he decided to phone Éditions Gallimard upon landing. Gallimard is Kundera's publisher, and surely, he thought, they could put the translator in touch with the author. Well, Gallimard soon burst the narcissistic bubble of our translator, by politely informing him of Kundera's absolute refusal to meet anyone.

Nonetheless, we all know that the stone walls of narcissism are never so easily broken.

Quite shaken by what he has just heard, my father responds: "But I am the translator of his works into Farsi!"

He continues: "In any case, this is my phone number, and my room number at my hotel. You tell Kundera that I never dreamed that he would be the kind of character who would refuse to meet the Farsi translator of his works," and he ends the conversation with the Gallimard representative.

Well, this is how the story unfolds: a few days later, the night before my father is due to leave Paris and a few minutes before he walks out of his room for a dinner engagement—all these insignificant coincidences!—his phone rings. My father picks up the phone and says: "Allo?" and wow—at the other end he hears a voice that, although he has never heard it before, he finds incredibly familiar. Kundera says: "C'est Milan Kundera," in his charming Czech accent.

My father runs downstairs. While he is running he thinks of Kundera reminding us, in *The Unbearable Lightness of Being*, that "Chance, and chance alone, has a message for us."

They talk for hours in the lobby of the hotel, and my father cancels his previous dinner engagement when he is invited to dine with the Kunderas at their home. Vera is elegant and hospitable; Milan shares his paintings, photos, and thoughts with my father; and the three of them become friends.

The Parisian evening comes to an end as my father walks back to his hotel room, absolutely safe in his now reconstructed narcissistic bubble.

I just called the translator of *The Unbearable Lightness of Being*, telling him I am trying to write a biographical novel. Without hesitation, he said: "You should read *The Art of the Novel.*"

I thought to myself: "How *dare* he?"

I have read every word Kundera has ever put on paper; he has been my secret vehicle for emotional communications; and yet he is referring me to him. Feeling agitated and misunderstood, I listened to what the translator had to say.

"You see, maybe you should write your diaries; maybe the title should be *The Diaries of a Psychoanalyst in Tehran*, for writing a novel is no easy task. One should only write a novel if one has something new to say that no one else can. It has to say something new in regard to the ontology of the human condition; it should disturb the reader."

Why am I so provoked? How can he have such an influence on me? It physically affects me. My heart is beating fast, my body is very tense, and I cannot keep up with my breathing. All my years of analysis cannot rescue me from the effects provoked in me by the translator, but something has changed; I find myself reacting differently. I ask him if he wants to hear what I have written. He replies: "Absolutely."

Feeling like a child who is ice-skating, asking her parents to gaze at her, I start to read.

I am so focused on every noise coming through the telephone from the other end, any little word that might give me a clue to what is going through my father's mind. I am holding on to the phone so tightly, as if holding on for dear life. I am sweating, and my heartbeat is so fast now that I can hear it inside my head. The content of my writing has long since eluded me; I am giving it no attention.

At the end, in a very cool and nonchalant voice (for I refuse to acknowledge the extent of my preoccupation with his desire; not to myself, not to anybody, but most certainly not to him), I ask my father: "So what do you think?" He—kindly, but with his usual firm intonation—replies: "It is good."

Ah, the magic of words! His last sentence lifts all my anxiety; all my worries are translated into pure joy and ecstasy. Just these few words: "It is good." How strange that now they are just ink on paper; how impotent they seem. Although from my personal experience I know better. I am not fooled by their powerless façade; I am aware of their superpowers; words are humanity's most effective weapons.

Anything is possible using words: they can injure us like no weapon of mass destruction can; they can make us laugh; they can give us hope; they can disturb our entire belief systems; they can give us confidence; make us feel valuable. Even love owes everything to words, as Jacques Lacan tells us.

Of course, I am not awarding such potency to the actual word. We have learned from the Swiss linguist Ferdinand de Saussure of the absence of "dogginess" in the word "dog," or "treeness" within the word "tree." The relationship between signifier and signified is mediated by social consensus and decided by a linguistic community, and, if anything, is a shaky, unfixed relationship.

Lacan, following Saussure, has written that "the symbol manifests itself first as the murder of the thing." Here he is referring to the self-effacing nature of language, which essentially distorts that which it is attempting to clarify. This impossibility of a transcendental truth that exists, as it were, beyond language is what makes language an impossible medium for expression in any of its forms, since by its very nature language disappoints, and can only be a vehicle for *miscommunication*.

Because of this disappointment we are forced into the trap of attempting to find our way out of this ambiguity through the same medium of imperfect language, thus leaving us in perpetual lack or desire. Lacan writes: "The symbol manifests itself first of all as the murder of the thing, and this constitutes in the subject the externalization of his desire."

If I want to put it simply, it was not only the actual words my father verbalized that had such an enormous power over me: they were fueled with power because of who they were coming from and for whom they were intended, and because of the emotional relationship between the two subjects.

But why am I telling you this story, why such a desire to write so shortly after my arrival in Tehran? Why does it feel like such a necessity to write?

Am I telling you this story to conceal another? This would be a futile attempt on my part, for the only way you will access the story I am trying to avoid telling you is through the very attempt to hide it: through the narration of the current story. For every story we tell holds as one of its most important functions an attempt at hiding many other stories. Do we not talk to hide what we really want to say? But this is a futile attempt indeed, for it is impossible not to communicate. For, as Freud has taught us, "Flight is precisely an instrument that delivers one over to what one is fleeing from."

In *Ignorance*, Kundera talks at length about Odysseus, so I wonder: in Homer's books, did Odysseus tell his story in order to hide the real tale? Was Odysseus trying to hide his disappointment at his great return, to conceal how non-great a return it really was? Was he trying to hide his new-found nostalgia for Calypso, the same nostalgia that had been reserved for Penelope for twenty years? How confused must poor Odysseus have been? Nostalgia is the territory of the homeland, of where you started from; the audience desperately wants Odysseus home, near his familiar olive tree, where faithful Penelope has been waiting for him all these years. But what about Odysseus himself? Did he not miss the ecstasy he had tasted in Calypso's arms? Was he ashamed of feeling like a stranger in his own home?

That, I believe, is one of the most disillusioning, painful realizations of the human condition: finding that one does not even belong where one is supposed to belong.

If one inhabits but does not belong in a foreign land, that is not only tolerable but at some level pleasurable. One is able to eroticize the suffering, to flirt with one's image as the stranger, to become an exotic Other. But what happens if one feels like a stranger in one's own land? What if that is how Odysseus felt upon his return: not that he would want to go back and reverse the process of the great return, of course; but what did really happen to him, the greatest gate-keeper of nostalgia, having been betrayed by nostalgia? No wonder he told and told and told us about the Odyssey in such great detail. Unfortunate Odysseus must have had a lot to hide.

This mode of hiding is reminiscent of the child's ego-centric stage, when, according to Piaget, he is playing hide-and-seek. He closes his eyes in an attempt to hide, while all along the Other is watching him, yet he believes that merely because he cannot see the Other, the Other cannot see him either. He has the illusion of safety and feels that he will not be caught.

It is like escaping from the prison of the Other while the Other is sleeping—we are living in disguise. Perhaps this is a manifestation of the universal existential anxiety of the human condition, which creates a feeling of alienation. This is, I believe, a matter of fooling ourselves into being this imaginary subject living life in accordance with the desire of the Other, as opposed to the truth of our own desire, as Lacan says. It is about how we disguise ourselves behind these various roles, and the enslavement that accompanies such a state. In other words, human beings are in a perpetual state of feeling like frauds, under the illusion that they are fooling themselves and the Other.

These thoughts deliver me straight to my flight from Tehran to Boston a few weeks ago. I had by now become familiar with various realities about my homeland; realities I had heard about and believed I was prepared for. I was a well-analyzed subject, I thought, who had experienced ambivalence, who knew that things are never just good or bad, and I was not expecting paradise to be waiting for me upon my return.

But something strange happened when I arrived in Tehran after twenty years. I was taken by surprise. It seems that all my years of hard work and preparation had not prepared me for what I am about to report. It seems that I, the apparently well-analyzed subject, not only expected paradise after all, but also had very fixed ideas about how this paradise was going to treat me.

I have, however, spent years telling my patients, my friends, my family, myself, anybody who would lend me their ears, that we are all utterly alone; we are all bound to feel misunderstood; we can never find a place to which we truly belong. This is the human condition, and paradise is merely an infantile fantasy. How righteous I used to feel while verbalizing this discourse; how superior. I had understood Camus's vision of Sisyphus, and I was able to tolerate it; I was able to experience freedom and subjectivity because of it.

So where did all this intellectual discourse evaporate to? It seems that I had secretly hoped that none of it was true. How I had fantasized about my great return, when I would feel I belonged; my return to where people spoke my language, in the broader sense of the word. I was home, to live where I had lived before; I had finally arrived at my version of the olive tree.

How painful it has been to become disillusioned. My great native land was not the way I remembered it, and the person I had become was not the way people remembered me.

To return to my flight from Tehran to Boston: a few months after my own mediocre return, I went back to

Boston for a short visit. The plane was taking off, and it was night-time. I could see the city I had longed for all these years. The city that had taught me the meaning of nostalgia; the city of mountains unmatched anywhere else in the world, its stunning streets with ancient trees lining both sides; and yet in the months that had elapsed since my return I had not even remembered to look at the mountains.

I was furious at Tehran for keeping me in a state of longing all these years, only to end up disappointing me. I felt betrayed by Tehran, and yet while the plane was taking off, it suddenly all came back. I could not believe I was feeling nostalgic: I already missed Tehran; I could feel myself starting to reminisce, and it was as if the last few months had never happened. It was as if I had a sadomasochistic relationship with my memory; whatever my memory did to betray me I would find myself trusting it, only to feel abandoned by it all over again. And so, with my illusions about Tehran intact, I left Tehran.

Ms. N is late for her second session. As the minutes move away from 4 o'clock, my fantasies start to go wild. At 4:05, I think: last time she arrived 15 minutes early, and had to wait for me while I finished with another patient; this time, does she want me to be the one anticipating *her* arrival? At 4:10 I am still consoling myself with the thought that she wants to play hardball with me; by 4:15 all rhyme and reason abandons me, leaving nothing but anguish once again. It seems that anguish will be accompanying Ms. N and me every step of the way.

Is she not coming? I try to go through our last session in my head, finding that I read all her previous communications as clear indications of her desire to return. What did I miss? It has been many years since I have experienced such worries about a patient. What is going on with me?

Right at this moment the doorbell rings; I open the door to a very different-looking Ms. N. She looks lovely today: she has put on a crisp linen outfit, her hair is beautifully done, and she smells like a fresh spring day.

Soon after I open the door she informs me that her lateness is due to the horrible traffic in Tehran.

Not the traffic excuse, I think to myself.

I, like any other psychoanalyst, have heard "traffic resistance" a thousand times; it is our equivalent of "the dog chewed my homework." As a result, I find myself slightly annoyed and disappointed.

My ideal, intelligent, cultured, self-reflective, my extraordinary patient is using the most ordinary of excuses for her lateness.

In order to heal the pain of yet another disillusionment, I think of Kundera again. I remember that in his novel *Identity* the reader finds that Chantal, a brilliant, intellectual, and in a sense extraordinary woman, is responding with all the characteristics attributed to ordinary women to love letters from a secret admirer. We even find Kundera's highly sophisticated Chantal hiding her love letters under her lingerie; it cannot get any more ordinary than that, can it?

But I had still found Chantal extraordinary. Her ordinary act of hiding her love letters under her lingerie had not only at some level confirmed her femininity in my eyes (for I do not know any woman who does not hide her love letters under her lingerie, or at least fantasize about doing so); Chantal had also allowed me to become more comfortable with my own ordinariness, to be more accepting and forgiving of it.

And thus, with my newfound hope and this reminder of the ordinariness of the most extraordinary of characters, I showed Ms. N to the couch.

I had put my notebook on my chair to prevent an encore of the previous session; I was not going to get on the couch unless I was the one under investigation. But are both analytic subjects not under investigation at all times, are we not continuously also being analyzed by our patients? Would it not be a more fair indication of reality if the patient and I switched from the chair to the couch, each of us taking turns at both?

Before I continue with Ms. N's session, I would like to digress even further and associate to my relationship with someone else. For I feel it is time to introduce another of my master-signifiers, Professor S. I am reminded of him now, for I can hear his voice, with his charming intonations, with the warmth of his presence; I have always enjoyed referring to him as the "Psychoanalyst with a Heart." Right about now he would be saying: "Banal, not banal, ordinary, extraordinary, what does it all mean? Gohar, what is your preoccupation with extraordinary people anyway? I find ordinary people so much more interesting."

Instead of directly reporting on the history of my relationship with Professor S, I will ask you to discover the past through my account of its present state. How, after a very close and intense relationship lasting many years, during which time he performed various significant roles in my life and in my psychic organization, I had to leave Boston, and leave Professor S, to arrive at my version of the olive tree.

I saw him for the last time in his office, a space that embodied within it the remembrance of times past; where I had entered years back, a very different person to the one I am today. Where I had cried in front of him time after time, where I had learned from him, where he had become the only person in my life who had not invested in my passivity nor my femininity, where he had patiently and slowly shown me the roads toward subjectivity, where we had colluded together against the whole world when it was absolutely necessary, speaking only my mother tongue, even though I could only bear to use the lexicon of a second language.

Professor S had become my version of the olive tree away from my olive tree, and his office my transitional space, where I had found the safety and containment needed for any child to grow up.

I remember how I used to cherish those hours in his office with him, knowing that however I entered the room, I would always leave with newfound knowledge. Unlike the usual people lulling us with various illusions, Professor S always reminded me that you can't erase any kind of misery, but you can find out where it comes from through an investigation. This is the optimism of curiosity, of awareness, of questioning, as Julia Kristeva tells us so elegantly.

Ah, how he had mastered the art of being a teacher and a psychoanalyst with a heart! And no matter what kind of transference you had to him, you always felt understood when you left his presence.

As I was saying goodbye to him, fighting tears and feeling overwhelmed by all that I was feeling, I wanted to tell him so many things: how grateful I was, how I wished I could give him something in return for everything he had given me over the years, merely for the sheer pleasure he obtained from giving, never expecting anything back. How I appreciated his delicate way of introducing critiques; how I was going to miss him; how I was afraid of facing the world without his continuing guidance, wisdom, and clarity of thought. I did not utter a word, neither did he, but for the first time in the history of our relationship he took me in his arms and said "Goodbye."

I replied: "I will dearly miss you."

As I shut the door of his familiar office behind me, the door of what had become our space, mine and his, I kept repeating to myself what Freud told Theodor Reik on the occasion of their parting. He said that people need not be glued together if they belonged together. I kept repeating that phrase to heal the pain of saying goodbye to someone I knew I could never find in anyone else. I felt utterly grateful, and associated to Forough Farokhzad's poem "Someone Who Is Like No One":

> Someone who is like no one, not like Father, not like
>> Ensi, not like Yahya, not like Mother, and is
>> like the person who he ought to be.
> And his height is greater than the trees around the
>> overseer's house, and his face is brighter than
>> the face of the mahdi,
> And he's not even afraid of Sayyed Javad's brother who
>> has gone and put on a policeman's uniform.
> And he's not even afraid of Sayyed Javad himself who
>> owns all the rooms of our house.
> And his name just like Mother says it at the beginning
>> and at the end of prayers is either "judge of judges"
>> or "need of needs."

And with his eyes closed he can recite all the hard
    words in the third-grade book, and he can even take
    away a thousand from twenty million without
    coming up short.
And he can buy on credit however much he needs
    from Sayyed Javad's store. And he can do something
    so that the neon Allah sign which was as green as
    dawn will shine again in the sky above the
    Meftahiyan Mosque . . .

For reasons that are still an enigma to me, this is the
story I remembered as I closed the door:

With a smile on my face I remembered that one day, in
the middle of a severe Bostonian winter, I received a message from a supervisor informing me, in a very worried
voice, that I was in trouble, and asking me to call her back
immediately. This is how the message went:

"Call me back; you are in trouble."

As I listened to the message I became convinced that
I was going to face consequences and punishments for everything I had done wrong all my life. All those little things

that I was sure I had gotten away with, and all the grave sins I had committed.

I wanted to call her back and tell her: "Of course I am in trouble, do you know what I have done since I was a little girl? Did people finally see through my fraud?" (This is the fraud I was referring to earlier.)

That day I thought I was going to get into trouble for all my sins, including the colorful little soaps my brother and I had taken from a store when we were little kids.

Carrying on my shoulders what felt like the burden of humanity's sins, I dragged myself to the only place I would always end up in such dire states. Where else but Professor S's office? It was a room of our own, where the compulsion to confess was always right with me.

I related the incident and informed him of my concerns about the sort of punishments that awaited me. He listened attentively and said: "Gohar, you are very guilty of many sins, especially of having had Oedipal, pre-Oedipal, and many other vicious fantasies. You are indeed sinister; however, you are not going to get into trouble for your sins today, I guarantee it. Call that person right now and put a stop to this nonsense." Neither of us was a bit surprised when my supervisor informed me that I had left my Kundera book, *Immortality*, in her office, and she was convinced that people who left their immortality behind must be in trouble.

My associations fully abandon my patient and take me further away from her to this morning when I had woken up to the Tehran sun.

This is one of the most treasured characteristics of my city: the sun is always there, every morning, like a faithful lover. I once asked a British friend: "Why did you choose to live in Tehran?"

She said: "Because of the sun; you people take it for granted. Do you know what it means for a Londoner to have sunny days, every day of the year, day in and day out? No, you do not know; you've always had it; you expect it, you do not even get disappointed if it is not there one day; you find the rain romantic. You say: 'Good, we have rain; the country needs water.' You know you can afford to make such grandiose comments because you know the sun always comes back to you. I hate the rain; I would rather watch my whole country dry up than ever see a drop of rain again.

Does that answer your question? I moved to Tehran for the sun! I do not want any of the privileges London has to offer if it means having to tolerate rain, rain, and more rain."

In a sense the Londoner was right. It seems Iranians tend to eroticize death, mourning, sadness, and depression, encapsulated in rain. I wonder if it could have to do with our Oedipus, a boy named Sohrab?

Our famous myth "Rustam and Sohrab," from Ferdousi's *Book of Kings* (*Shahnameh*), has a storyline quite similar to that of *Oedipus Rex*, the main difference being that it is the father who unknowingly kills his son at the end. Greek mythology seems to be populated with myths about killing fathers, while it is impossible to escape the common pattern of killing sons all over Iranian mythology.

I am convinced of the universality of the Oedipus complex, and the struggle for power and control it represents while embodying within itself the universal fear of castration; however, the culturally specific element seems to be the reaction to this fear. My premise is that the Iranian collective fantasy is anchored in an anxiety of disobedience that wishes for an absolute obedience. The sons, while desiring to rebel, know unconsciously that if they do so they might get killed, and so in a way they settle for the fear of castration. I find that this is characteristic of traditional cultures.

We know that laws are developed as a reaction, to solve certain problems in society. Hence, within the history of Iran, we can again see the demand for absolute obedience as a reaction formation to the anxiety of the potential rebelliousness of the culture (in this case the sons). So, ironically, this culture of absolute obedience on the surface is indeed a rebellious one internally.

Meanwhile, Greek culture seems to be about taking over and substituting power, the collective fantasy allowing deviation from and elimination of the father in response to the fear of castration, in order to gain power and control.

This means essentially that laws in Iran are followed as long as the police, the law, and the father are present. If not, within this culture of no rebellion, every rebellious act becomes possible. Is this not also seen in the differences between Catholicism and Islam? Islam means submission, and demands absolute obedience to God the father, while in Christianity the demarcation between God the father and Christ the son is not quite as clear. It seems as though religions were socially constructed to fulfill the collective fantasies of these differing cultures. An analysis of Iranian history reveals that it has constantly been a one-man show, while democracy was born within and is the essence of Greek society.

In Iran one can observe a moment of discontinuity from the past, and also from the future, because we have killed our sons, our future. Ferdousi's discourse communicates a lot of pain, tragedy, and mourning. We killed our sons, became alienated, and thus became a culture of mourning, for we destroyed and killed the best part of ourselves. We destroyed our future and imprisoned ourselves in the past, eroticizing pain and suffering, and celebrating nothing that is not past.

Could we say that Ferdousi's discourse provides a diagnosis of Iranian society? He is trying to warn us, awaken us; his discourse is that of a depressive.

We never properly mourned the loss of our glorious past, before it was taken over by Islam. Our melancholic response was to create Shiism, which is a culture of mourning, as a way of mourning the symbolic past. Through this ever-repetitive mourning we attempt to master the sudden trauma of having suddenly lost our sense of who we are.

Daryoush Shaygan informs us that the Iranian past is full of myths and epics represented in the *Shahnameh*, where there are continual allusions to the good attitude of our ancestors, the beliefs and actions of our heroes, and the myths of our great kings. This is a very nostalgic recollection; in a sense, a very nostalgic collective unconscious.

One has to bear in mind that in countries like Iran the past is everything, and unfortunately we do indeed breathe the air of regrets, as Shaygan puts it. At the risk of disturbing the Londoner, I have to confess that I found the sun depressing this morning; the brightness of the Tehranian sun would not allow me to escape where I was, for it immediately reminded me of where I had landed.

The experience of guilt caused by not appreciating the sun brings me back to my session with Ms. N, who had started it by telling me: "Because of my arthritis I had to go to the hospital a few months ago. I am telling you this story because the whole experience brought me humility and even more love for my people. Everybody was so warm, so caring. OK, they were on my case all the time; they would not allow me five minutes of calm to read my book, but I felt more alive in that hospital room in Tehran than I have felt in the most beautiful, luxurious hotels in the world. You know our people: Iranians have a lot of faults, but we are soft, the absolute opposite of French people."

I found myself feeling a great deal of guilt, but what had I done to feel guilty about? Was I feeling guilty because I did not find people particularly soft in my homeland? I did not feel as if I belonged with them; I found the hospitals chaotic, not soft. I preferred the distance I could keep from people in the West, especially if I wanted to be left alone, or get some work done. Everybody seems so warm and caring here, but is that not just an excuse to drink tea with each other and justify our laziness? I do not want to become lazy.

What am I saying? For twenty years, away from Tehran, I complained nonstop to my friends from all over the world about how much I missed the kind of contact and intimacy that relationships seem to enjoy in the East. Just like Ms. N, I hated the coldness—the *nothingness*, in a sense—that accompanied all of our lives in the West. There was nobody more Iranian than me outside of Iran and nobody less Iranian than me in Iran; as it is, I have trouble recognizing myself now. Where has all my steadfast love for my country gone? What am I to do with this new knowledge about myself: the mirage that has been taken away from me, while behind it I had to come face to face with myself as an absolutely nonpatriotic citizen?

Maybe in the West people suffer from an unbearable lightness of being, while in the East it is the heaviness that becomes unbearable.

Are we bound to feel guilty if we are not absolutely enchanted with our homelands? Are we to torture ourselves because we have, in a sense, left the *mother*land, and we can never quite go back? Are we supposed to feel that we have betrayed our *mothers*, for we have come to agree with Proust, who says: "it seems the only real paradises are the ones we have lost"? Is it that if we are not suffering because of our homelands, we are cruel betrayers of our *mother*lands?

It seems we are destined to suffer guilt if we have become incapable of seeing our *mother*land as flawless, and have recognized that our paradise is nowhere to be found, especially not in our homeland, and that our paradise is forever lost. This, however, is the matricide needed if any child is to develop a mind, as Melanie Klein has elaborated, according to Julia Kristeva's reading of her: "In order to think one must first lose the mother."

Let us go back to Ms. N as she is trying to convince me of the enchantments of our city. (I wonder at this point whom she is really trying to convince? Me or herself? For I have learned that what people say they want is never what they really want. Also that as neurotics we are always saying what we do not mean.)

Ms. N continues: "Let me give you an example: I lived in my apartment building in Paris for twenty-three years; not even once did one of my neighbors knock on my door. We all lived there for years and knew nothing about each other, absolutely nothing. I always thought about the horror of one of our bodies rotting for months in an empty apartment, where it would start to reek like a corpse: the body surrounded by insects, each taking little pieces to feed themselves. Maybe there would even be a cat taking the eyeballs out and using them as toys, throwing them around, leaving traces of blood all over the place. Until the disgusting odor would lead to someone remembering: 'Oh, there are other people in this building.' Yes, only through the death of a neighbor would we be reminded that once upon a time they existed, that they were alive. Before that we would have absolutely no use for or any interest in our neighbors' lives.

"You know, Doctor, on the other hand, one week after moving to Iran, I could no longer manage to get any work done. All my projects fell behind, and I submitted myself without the slightest resistance to the ways of the East. It was as if all these years of punctuality, hard work, and immaculate organization were vehicles to deliver me to this desired destination, where half of my time was spent entertaining one of my neighbors who would show up unannounced, bringing me sweets, food, or fruits from a grandfather's village, and the rest of my time was taken up with thinking about putting something in their now empty pots, plates, and baskets and knocking on their doors unannounced to return their kindheartedness.

"Of course each knock on the door would end up in an invitation for coffee or tea with more sweets, food, and fruits from a grandfather's village.

"Everybody in Tehran seems to be knocking on everybody else's door, unannounced, all the time.

"I love it; this is life, and this is the softness I was referring to. You are probably thinking it's a cliché, but that does not make it any less valid.

"I hate the loneliness, the individualism, the lack of human relationships and contact that is not particular to France, but that I have found to be a general characteristic of the West. People are a lot less lonely in the East, and they smile more than in the West—this is a fact I personally know to be true. There is such a different quality to loneliness in the East. I suppose this is why there is such a hyperreal desire for souvenirs of the East in the West. And so in recent years Westerners have started to aspire to the simplicity and the slowness of time in the East through meditation, yoga, and Buddhism. You see, something is not working in the West, for they are seeking something to smile about in the East."

I find myself torn by my superego shouting in my head: "You are the analyst, listen to what she is saying, to whom she is saying it, and why now? What is she trying to communicate? Think about her internal psychic need for the split between us and them: the East as the all-encompassing source of goodness, the very good and soft breast, while the West represents all that is toxic, dangerous, inhumane, cruel; indeed, the bad breast." My superego's voice is instructing me to think of my patient in terms of denial, splits, projections, and other forms of defense. Telling me to try to understand her unconscious fantasy, and . . . Does she want me to collude with her? Two Iranian women, from different generations, both recently returned to the *mother*land?

But there is a part of me that does not want to listen to her discourse with an analytic ear; I want to get into a discussion with her. I want to say: "Listen, Ms. N. OK, there are things that don't work in the West, but do you consider the East a place where things are functioning? Oh please; look at India, where all the yogis in the world are not able to stop hunger. Or have you tried the post office in Tehran, or the bank? No, they are not working." I do not want to stop here: I want to say to Ms. N: "Do you know what happened to me yesterday?"

Yesterday I found myself in a famous psychiatric hospital in Tehran, where I was really impressed and, I have to admit, surprised by the degree of organization I observed. While I am waiting for the psychoanalyst with whom I have a meeting (he is an hour late, probably because he is having tea with his neighbor), and due to a great number of patients just signing up that day, I find myself with two files in my hand in an office with a very big woman in front of me, holding her tiny one-year-old daughter in her arms.

I decide to rise to the occasion: I ask her why she is here. She responds hysterically, crying, shouting, hitting herself, while all the time the one-year-old girl is silent. As the mother gets more and more hysterical, and I find myself not comprehending a word of what she is saying, the look on the baby's face begins to grow calmer. The mother is shouting and I am not hearing a single word, while the silence of the one-year-old is being heard by me loud and clear. For it is true that if we want to be heard we do not shout but whisper, as Theodore Rilke reminds us.

The chubby mother demands a letter from me to enforce her husband's hospitalization. After looking at the husband's file, seeing that he suffers from both addiction and schizophrenia, while observing the begging eyes of the quiet child, who in my opinion is whispering: "Just give my mother the damn letter, so I can have a moment of peace," I agree to give her the letter.

We all walk to the office of the head of the hospital, a man who has become part of the legends told about this hospital, for while he is paid very little, he has managed to work for forty years, nonstop, with the heart of an Easterner and the mind of a Westerner. He is on time, organized, and empathic with every single patient in this hospital. Having heard of his reputation, I take my case to him and demand a letter on behalf of my chubby patient and her silent little girl.

He looks at me with wide-open eyes, with surprise and even a little envy of my absolute unawareness of the circumstances of this hospital. In a voice I can barely hear because it is so soft, the legend utters the following words: "My dear Doctor, what if I write the letter, and when he is brought here we do not have an empty bed? Should I take him home with me?"

My patient, it seems, does not need my advocacy, for right away she responds to him: "Well, what am I supposed to do? Have him stay in the house and beat me up all day and night?" The doctor of the legends of Tehran responds to the chubby woman's very legitimate question: "You know, my child, we should both have been born in Sweden; under those conditions we would be talking to each other on completely different terms."

I feel like an outsider; they seem to understand each other's language, while for me they might as well be speaking Swedish.

The chubby woman, now calm and relaxed, responds: "If you look at the map, Sweden is not even that far from Iran."

The legend replies to her: "My darling wise girl, do not envy them, for, statistics inform me, all the privileges they have been granted does not seem to stop a large number of them from committing suicide." They both laugh, the woman and the little girl are both smiling; the doctor is offering sweets and tea now, as though all of their thoughts are far from empty beds and Swedish people.

In order to join in with their wonderfully coordinated dance, to include myself, I say: "Why don't you write the letter, while emphasizing that it is contingent upon having an empty bed."

He says: "Will do, Doctor, will do. Let us finish our tea."

While this story was meant to remind you of everything that is not working in the East—and that should be crystal clear—paradoxically, it also conveys precisely what Ms. N is describing, the thing which seems to be lacking in the West, the thing which the heart of an Easterner has mastered.

Here I am reminded of Pande, quoted in Salman Akhtar's book *Immigration and Identity*:

> For the East, relatively speaking, past, present, and future merge into one another; for the West they are discrete entities. For the East, experience in time is like water collected in a pool (stagnant, perhaps); for the West, time is more like water flowing in a stream, and one is acutely aware that what flows away, flows away forever.

Ms. N continues: "I know all my neighbors' stories now. I know that Mr. F on the third floor, who is not married, is rarely home and is part of the known intellectual circles of Tehran.

"He has a very unique sense of humor and makes his money doing intellectual work, which, as everybody knows, is a path toward poverty! I always thought that if it might be justified for somebody to be a Marxist, it would be Mr. F. And yet, bringing me fresh bread yesterday, he reacted very angrily to my Che Guevara poster!

"He said: 'You come from a rich, aristocratic family and yet you have a Che poster; why don't you people at least know that Che and his buddies are particularly bad for the likes of you; why don't you at least understand that your rights and your lifestyle are at risk because of people like him; why don't you people know at least what is good for you, and what threatens your well-being?

"'If the workers are Marxists, OK, that is more digestible. But you, why don't you think? How can you admire and follow an ideology that interferes with all that you adhere to? And please do not tell me it is for humanitarian reasons: that you are sacrificing your own privileges for those less fortunate than you are! I do not believe in any sort of altruism, and if only we all consciously followed what was good for us, we would have a much more pleasant and civilized world to live in.

"'Because of your ridiculous poster I have changed my mind; do not introduce me to any women; I do not want to be introduced to somebody eccentric, strange, or different. I want somebody who likes to eat caviar, who enjoys good wine, who appears clean-cut and does not associate intellectualism with wearing no lipstick, not getting her nails done, and not taking showers.

"'People of Tehran, please hear me: May 68 is long over; acting as if those days are alive today is the epitome of banality. You can wear heels, you can enjoy money, luxury, and comfort, and you can wear nail polish and lipstick while being an intellectual, if that is what you desire.

"'The crucial thing is to be authentic: be who you are, for everybody else is already taken. And if you do not act upon your own desire, you are bound to be a prisoner; the only variable is who your prison guard is. One day your prison guard enforces lipstick as the enemy, while another day the guard informs you that all intellectuals must wear red lipstick. If there is any possibility of minimizing enslavement, it is through following our own desire, and so becoming who we are.

"'What does it mean to be an intellectual anyway? These categories are not fixed, they are agreed upon between specific groups of people; they vary, they are relative, and they do not mean the same thing across cultures.

"'Do not categorize people as nonintellectuals because they drive expensive cars; this is only about the lack, the void, the stupidity you feel inside, which you project onto them. I have begun to despise the intellectuals of this city; they feel as if they cannot walk on the sidewalk like everybody else, they have to walk through the dirtiest, most difficult of roads and come out smelling like sweat in their old shoes. That is what it means to be an intellectual to them. How pathetic they appear to me! Why can't they walk on the sidewalk so they can actually get somewhere, anywhere? Maybe it is because they have nothing to do, to teach, to say; maybe because without this façade of old shoes, unshaven beards, strange behavior, they have to come face to face with their own banality; maybe it is their defense against realizing they are nobodies. And not just any nobodies; smelly nobodies with long oily hair.

"'Do not introduce me to anybody like that, please; introduce me to somebody who is not banal.'"

I, the analyst, am very aroused and stimulated by my patient's discourse; I find Mr. F's anger very authentic, his language passionate. I could also hear a kind of suffering in his voice, which seems to be what binds the three of us: Ms. N, Mr. F, and me. Banality, for various reasons of our own, tortures us all.

I want to hear more about Mr. F, and his hatred for banality is touching something very close to my own fear of it, so I say nothing, terrified that any word from me might break Ms. N's narrative.

She continues: "Banality is interesting, no? I told Mr. F that banality surrounds us all; it is everywhere. It is not just in Tehran; it is not just this group of people you are talking about who suffer from banality. I warned him that banality is taking over the world like videogames.

"Mr. F and I feel truly checkmated by banality; what are we to do? We are feeling more and more alone; there are so many people infected with banality, so few of us left untouched.

"Mr. F told me that banality knows neither color, gender, nor class; banality is moving across cultures. Banality is a populist."

Ms. N asked her friend: "But what about the few who have not been affected by it? This could be a clue for us. If only we could figure out how they escaped the poisonous venom of banality, we might be able to make an antidote for the disease; we might be able to save people from banality?"

"Mr. F said: 'I have already questioned this small group of people. I asked them: "How come you have been safe from the ever-seductive trap of banality?"

"'They all find this problem and this kind of discourse quite banal: they are bored by this problem, they have better things to do, and I am finding our discourse quite banal right now.'"

Having momentarily become an integral part of the dialog between Ms. N and Mr. F, having experienced their desperation, I want to offer them the only solution I have for anything, so, impulsively, and in order to escape the hopelessness brought into the session, I say: "Why don't you get banality psychoanalyzed? *Put banality on the couch.* As long as banality is being investigated, as long as banality is being questioned, I can assure you there is hope."

She calmly continues: "Mr. F and I have been safe until now, and I have no doubt that we are very well shielded from banality, no matter how strong or powerful it gets. *You* just have to solve the riddle of what it is that shields us from banality. Think, think, and think."

I find myself irritated now; did my patient just categorize me as banal? I am very frustrated at how the session is going; I think to myself: has Ms. N succeeded once again in throwing me out of the analyst's chair, by seducing me with her interesting discourse? I had become so fascinated by her discourse that I had stopped thinking like a psychoanalyst. I did not wonder why she was telling me her story about Mr. F, why she was bringing him into our relationship when she did. And what was going on with me that I had drifted so far away from her into my own thoughts: as a defense? Why did I start bringing Professor S into the session when I did? Did I need his guidance?

And why am I so preoccupied with my position as an analyst anyway? Why can I not let myself enjoy this fascinating patient, who is performing her only required task as a patient, and talking?

I promise myself that I will concentrate on her discourse as an analyst; I straighten myself up, fix my glasses, and try to listen to her with a "third ear," as an analyst must.

Although for years now I have considered myself the poster child for postmodernity, it seems I am absolutely incapable of allowing myself to break away even for a minute from what has come to signify being a psychoanalyst within my psychic structure.

I ask Ms. N what a nonbanal person represents for her.

She quickly replies: "After many years of thinking about this question, I have found one difference between those I categorize as banal and those who are not banal: non-banal people like myself have taken their destiny by the balls and into their own hands; we have assumed subjectivity; we do not believe things happen to us; we consider ourselves responsible for the consequences of our actions; we are not victims, we choose, we have consciousness.

"Otherwise I have to tell you that there is absolutely not a bit of difference between people. Maybe some of us own a couple of pairs of shoes more than others. You see, it seems I have a thing with shoes; I use shoes as my preferred mode of explaining issues all the time."

I find myself being slowly seduced into her way of talking again. I like what she says and how she is saying it, but I am a little anguished, for I am, slowly, somehow of my own accord this time, unplugging my analytic ear. Maybe Ms. N is not the one removing me from my position, but I'm the one who is doing all the work. I am absolutely fascinated by her, and I would like to have dinner with her and Mr. F. I would like to become friends with them; I am the one who does not want her as a patient. This thought anguishes me; and so I give her a typical analytical line.

"Could you elaborate on what you are saying?"

"As a matter of fact, I wanted to tell you a few stories about my weekend trip to Shiraz with a few students of mine who are painters.

"My God, this country is beautiful, the architecture is breathtaking. In Shiraz one is reminded of how old Iran is, how rich the culture, how ancient the poetry. And I can never do justice with mere words to what it is like to visit Shiraz in spring.

"Throughout the whole trip I was reminded of the faithfulness of spring, how it has never betrayed me in Iran; it always arrives on time, and brings with it everything that it has promised. The blossoms and their maddening odors, singing birds, light showers of rain, and more blossoms. In spring Shiraz is taken over by the perfume of orange blossom. Spring in many parts of this country lives up to one's fantasy of an ideal spring. In Iran spring encompasses all that the wildest imaginations demand of it and make it out to be.

"But, Doctor, why do you think I find spring so very depressing? Is it because it comes full force, imposing itself upon you? Is it because one cannot do anything to ignore it, to get away from it? It really feels like being hijacked; no, more like being raped. Maybe I find it depressing because through spring, we are forced to face everything that represents life, birth, youth, while we are so intensely aware of getting older, and approaching death. You know that Simone de Beauvoir remarks: 'It is old age, rather than death, that is to be contrasted with life. Old age is life's parody, whereas death transforms life into a destiny: in a way it preserves it by giving it the absolute dimension. Death does away with time.' And so, because of spring's inevitable association to life, one cannot escape its absolute contrast, old age.

"Do I sound crazy to you, Doctor? I do not mind if I do. Have you seen the Buñuel movie *Belle de jour*? At the end, they leave the scene in a big carriage with *dum dum dum* in the background! That is how I would like to leave the scene, *dum, dum, dum*."

I, the analyst, for my part, find myself completely seduced by her discourse; I am clearly done for because Ms. N has put a hold on me like the one she claims she possesses over her destiny.

Ms. N goes on: "One day at a local restaurant in Shiraz I saw a group of women who were all covered in black chadors, can you imagine? All black in the midst of the spring day I just described to you. I decided to join their table; I sat with them around their table and wondered aloud: 'How come you are in black from head to toe? Does anybody force you to be so? You know black is the worst color to wear, it takes all the heat in, no color or light can find a way through it, while white is the opposite; could you explain to me why you are not covering yourselves in white on such a lovely spring day?' The women looked at me, and then finally the oldest one, in a very distant tone of voice, replied: 'Madam, you might be speaking very eloquent Farsi, much better than us, and yet it is obvious from listening to you that your language skills are not strong enough to understand us. We might both be speaking Farsi, yet you do not understand me and I do not understand you. We speak very different languages.' You see, Doc, she was not banal."

Although I enjoy Ms. N's story, her last lines remain like a knife in my heart. I have enough of the psychoanalyst surviving in me to hear the message Ms. N is trying to communicate to her analyst: that at some level she feels *we* do not understand each other, that *we* do not speak each other's language. My ideal patient's message is loud and clear: she does not experience me as an ideal analyst.

Like a wounded lover, I tell her we should stop for today. As Ms. N is about to leave (perhaps she knows at some level what she has communicated, and that indeed the message has got to the receiver), with what I perceive to be some degree of guilt, and in order, I believe, to repair the relationship, she hands me a small delicate lily of the valley from her big yellow bag and says: "I forgot I had brought this for you, I picked it from my own garden."

Perplexed at what has just happened, without much contemplation, I say "Thank you," as Ms. N leaves my office for that day.

I do not explore Ms. N's gesture, for not only was she standing up, marking the termination of the session, but also, to tell the truth, the lily of the valley's timely appearance has slightly healed my desperate realization of not having been an ideal analyst for my ideal patient. I, like the most ordinary of characters, thought to myself: "Oh, she likes me; she has brought me flowers from her garden."

I am well aware that more sophisticated analysts would have asked various questions, such as "What have I done to deserve a flower?" or even rejected it, informing the patient that they would have to talk about what the gesture represents in their psychic organization as well as their analytic dyad. Many psychoanalysts would have found the inevitable anxiety produced by the rejection or questioning of the patient's gesture a desirable place from which to learn more about various aspects of the patient, including her threshold for tolerating anxiety. A more sophisticated analyst would have seen some negativity on the part of the patient in the flower, and would not jump to evaluate the gesture as solely a libidinal one, as I did. My impulsive acceptance of the flower could also be considered a process of acting out on the part of the analyst to reduce her own anxiety. The situation leaves itself open to various other refined modes of investigation.

Professor S once informed me that as long as one was thinking about what had happened, what had been done and what the patient had said in a psychoanalytic manner, then that was psychoanalysis.

Perhaps just in order to redeem myself, please allow me to ponder upon the reasons for my impulsive acceptance of the lily of the valley and my immediate "Thank you" that followed it.

In the spirit of psychoanalysis, if we go back to my line of thought right before Ms. N handed me the lily, we are confronted by these words on the part of the analyst: "Her last lines remain like a knife in my heart. I have enough of the psychoanalyst surviving in me to hear the message Ms. N is trying to communicate to her analyst: that at some level she feels *we* do not understand each other, that *we* do not speak each other's language. My ideal patient's message is loud and clear: she does not experience me as an ideal analyst."

Did I welcome the arrival of the lily to console myself? Did I use the flower to take the knife out of my heart? Perhaps in order to transform a bloody situation of disappointment into a flowery condition of hope; as a vehicle to eliminate the anxiety of the former situation. Was I so desperate for my ideal patient to experience me as an ideal analyst as well? So desperate that the arrival of the lily of the valley, which also happens to be my favorite flower, left the space open for the possibility of such hopeful fantasy?

Yes, I adore the lily of the valley because I believe that each tiny little flower carries a secret, and I am convinced that it is the answer to what it means to be a woman. I find the lily of the valley to be the quintessential feminine. It has comfortably *made* itself a passive object, which, as Simone de Beauvoir teaches us, is very different from *being* a passive object. For the process of making oneself into a passive object encompasses in it choice and subjectivity, while being a passive object is what one believes to be one's destiny. It carries with it a lack of consciousness and of freedom.

The lily of the valley parallels the beauty of an orchid while being less imposing, less in your face. Its treasures are more hidden; you have to search for them; and unlike the orchid, which has put all its effort into its appearance, betraying itself in the realm of perfume, the lily of the valley, though extremely small, dominates the whole room as soon as it enters with its delicate but everlasting odor. Due to its fragrance one is absolutely incapable of ignoring the lily of the valley; one is continually made to become aware of it.

The lily of the valley, in psychoanalytic terminology, is like a good hysteric in her everlasting attempt to successfully seduce the Other, for it is only in the space occupied by the desire of the Other that the hysteric can ensure her continued existence.

Now how could I operate as an analyst, when my ideal patient surprised me with my beloved flower, with a lily of the valley, the reservoir of all my fantasies but, most importantly, my projections of all that I have categorized over the years under *what it means to be a woman*?

I think I am slowly becoming aware of why I resorted to a simple thank you.

Something else is also imposing itself on my line of associations: "culture." I have in my analytic career found it easy to reject and question my patients' gifts, letters, demands to look at their photos, etc. . . . Each time I thought about what should be done according to the specificity of the case and acted appropriately, always staying faithful to understanding what the meaning behind such an act might be, and trying to hear the message that the patient wanted to communicate through the act.

In Iran I found myself incapable of rejecting a box of sweets an older female patient brought me the other day. I am much more uncomfortable talking about the fee, asking the patients to take the couch, telling them that we are out of time. But why? Is it because speaking Farsi triggers different internal objects in me? Is it because Iranian culture, in the complete sense of the word, embodies within it a very different audience for me: the different others to whom I speak and who respond to me? For modern linguistics takes the spoken word to be a unique symbolic capsule containing developmental history. The spoken word is the story of the self, its desires, and its stories about the past and present objects of those desires.

Mikhail Bakhtin did not conceive of linguistic expressions as external copies of some internal representation. Meaning, for him, was not primarily inside or outside, but in constant flux between the two. He emphasized the way in which language, mind, and world are continually in interaction: each transforming the other. Word meaning, as Bakhtin would assert, is shaped in dialogs, whether with other people or with one's own impulses.

For Bakhtin, the inherently dialogic quality of human speech has not been fully appreciated. He asserts that this dialog is the subject of any utterance as much as its thematic content. Basically, what marks the distinction between languages may not be a particular vocabulary or grammar. As Wittgenstein notes:

One human being can be a complete enigma to another. We learn this when we come into a strange country with entirely strange traditions; and, what is more, even given a mastery of the country's language. We do not understand the people. (And not because we do not know what they are saying to themselves.) *We cannot find our feet with them.*

Thus it is not what the actual words in Farsi say that made my transition to being a psychoanalyst in Tehran difficult, but the way in which the words create various sensations in me, and the fantasies they trigger in me. One clear fantasy triggered seems to be: respect your elders; do not reject their gifts.

In short, I would say that one of the things that has made my return so turbulent has been that I have not yet succeeded in finding my feet with people in Tehran.

Today Ms. N shows up for her last session before her greatly anticipated three-week trip to Paris. She is dressed in a canary-yellow dress and uses a playful tone of voice; she throws herself on the couch effortlessly, carefully situating one foot on the couch and the other on the floor. She immediately says: "Mrs. Gohar . . ." (This is the first time she has referred to me by my first name instead of her usual "Doctor," or "Dr. Homayounpour.") "I am very tired today and I have the sentiments I usually have when I am leaving Tehran for Paris; you know that feeling of excitement, the feeling of adventures to come, of possibilities. I miss Paris and everything that it encompasses."

I ask her what she particularly misses about Paris.

"What I miss the most is myself. I do not even know what I just said signifies, but what comes to mind is paintings; you know I live and breathe paintings, they are where I experience the utmost pleasure and ecstasy. In Paris I am surrounded by paintings everywhere, from museums to galleries, while here my life lacks paintings. As far as I am concerned, Jesus sacrificed his body in the name of Western painting. OK, there are some other parts of Christianity used in Western painting, but it is predominantly Jesus' body that constitutes Western art. For me pleasure comes from painting, and the unique form of suffering I am willing to endure is the torture of creativity.

"Have you ever heard this assertion that it is Jesus' body that gave us Western painting, Mrs. Gohar, or do you not know much about art, although you are a symbolic communications expert?"

I feel inadequate and clumsy. What if I do not know enough about art after all? I am also tired today; I do not want a tennis match. She calls me by my first name; the unconscious language of her body has revealed to me that she already has one foot out the door, while she is now accusing me of ignorance about art, and implying that I suffer from a *déformation professionelle*, that I am one of those characters who is capable of deriving pleasure solely from her own profession, caricatured by my "symbolic communications" expertise.

I want to say: "Lady, you are the one that can get pleasure only from paintings; now stop projecting your feelings of inadequacy onto me. Stop using the defense of grandiosity to cover up the poor little girl shouting for her inaccessible mother." I want to say: "In one session you go on about the coldness of French people, and today you are bemoaning the lack of art and sophistication you endure in Tehran. What happened to the pleasures of knowing your neighbors' stories? What happened to the unmatchable charms of the Orient, and the Occident's lack of humanity?"

But what is going on with me? Why am I so angry and judgmental? I am well aware that her idealization and devaluation of Tehran are two sides of the same coin (as any idealization and devaluation are), so why am I tempted to turn into a cruel and judgmental object?

Thankfully my knowledge of psychoanalysis allows me to distance myself from the situation, and not to let our interpersonal dynamics turn me into the cruel and sadistic mother she has previously unconsciously depicted.

I am reminded of her parting-ship dream, when she is overcome by anxiety because she is incapable of fully dressing herself, often not being able to find a pair of her shoes. Is the excitement about the impending trip to which she has just referred another way of revealing to me her raw anxiety about separation, now magnified by our coming break? It seems to me that Ms. N is not equipped (or properly dressed) to separate from the object against the backdrop of a calm sea; separation as reported in her dream is the aftermath of a disaster followed by severe anxiety, devastating stormy seas, and no proper clothing. What a torturous image; truly the image of Jesus sacrificing his body, tormented, anguished, suffering, and, indeed, without proper clothing.

The sacrifice of one's body also leads me to think of her arthritis; in a sense she has sacrificed her body to arthritis, but for whose sins, her own or the Other's? And what is the grand sin that has been committed?

I am tempted to try to calm the sea represented by the format of our session, but I have a pretty firm conviction that we must go through this process together, that I have to tolerate the parting and separation on a very stormy note, to feel exactly how it feels to be Ms. N, to identify then empathize with her, and to show her I can tolerate and contain these torturous feelings. On that note, I respond to her question about whether I know much about art or whether I am a mere "symbolic communications" junky.

"Suppose I don't know anything about art: tell me everything you want to say about it."

Ms. N replies, in a very angry and loud tone of voice: "Why can't we have an ordinary conversation about something normal like art? You know, maybe you cured me too fast; now I am aware that I can just come here and tell my stories and nothing will change, that you are not here to help me and coming here will not lessen my pain or solve my problems. I ought to just come here for self-knowledge; that is what psychoanalysis is about, *à la* Aristotle, is it not? He, like you people, believed that a life not examined is a life not worth living. I agree, but frankly, Madam, I am done examining. I have done it all my life; I just want to look at paintings and, as I mentioned before, the only suffering I am willing to endure is the unavoidable suffering of creating art; I do not want to suffer for self-knowledge."

I am the one feeling anguished now: what can I say? Part of what she is saying makes logical sense to me, but I hold on to the assertion that separation has to be traumatic for Ms. N: this is the only mode of functioning she possesses before she leaves for three weeks. So, trying to tolerate the motion sickness of the stormy sea, I stay silent.

Ms. N continues: "Last time I was here, I came upon a small store near your office that sharpens knives, so right now my bag is full of knives that I am taking to the store to get sharpened. I did not want to tell you about them until the end of the session because I did not want to frighten you, remembering how intrigued you are by symbolic communications, but don't be scared. Our time is almost up."

Without any hesitation I say: "It seems we have moved from flowers to knives. I must have done something wrong."

Ms. N replies: "I admire your ability to take responsibility for the current sharp and knifelike situation we are in; you are not as flowery as you look after all."

After Ms. N's departure I am unable to get her out of my mind. Was she letting me know about her tortured self through the image of a tortured Christ betrayed and crucified for other people's sins? However, at the moment I am the one who is tormented; I feel that she is never coming back, and that I have lost her because I did not know enough about art. I was careless enough to have transformed my lily of the valley, my intelligent, ideal patient, into a woman with knives and crucifixes.

But theory yet again comes to my rescue, reminding me that I had possibly been a carrier of all that she was feeling, that these must be Ms. N's feelings, and that she could not have left for a break under any other conditions. It seems that Ms. N is not psychically equipped to undergo a separation that does not entail a violent trauma.

It does not come as a surprise that the thought of separation leads my associations to my own mother, for can any of us be reminded of separation without thinking of separation from our mother, where our most treasured dyadic relationship is violently taken from us?

My mother is like Romain Gary's mother. Romain Gary himself told us about a trip he took to Sweden with his mother during which they happened to pass a park where the king was playing tennis. The mother, desperate for her son to play tennis with the king, performed various tricks, including lying to the king's guards about her son's professional tennis qualifications. After many hours of the poor mother's various charades, the king agreed to a match with her son, only to find him entirely incompetent. In his own words, Romain Gary told us of his enormous but inadequate efforts to at least hit one single ball, while his mother watched him very proudly, without blinking; purely in order, I assume, to later spread the news of her son's marvelous tennis match with the king of Sweden.

My mother is, in a sense, like Romain Gary's mother. I remember it as though it happened yesterday: getting us ready for school every morning, my mother would whisper in my ear: "You are my favorite," while also reassuring my brother, into *his* ear, of the very same exceptional love.

It is not that my brother and I were not aware of what was going on, but we still played this game that seemed superbly pleasurable for all of us. The three of us knew very well what was happening and yet we played along, as in the story about the wife who has given up eating her favorite part of the chicken for fifty years, in order for her husband to have the part he likes best, the white meat, while her husband has been eating the white meat (the part he does not actually like) for fifty years, assuming he was the one making the ultimate sacrifice for love of his wife.

My line of associations takes me even further back. Many years ago my mother asked me if I knew why it was a great deal more important to be happy than to be rich, famous, and beautiful: because, as Schopenhauer informs us, if we are telling a friend about a very rich, famous, and attractive person, the first question we have to answer is: "But is he or she happy?" However, if we tell the tale of a happy person we are never asked if they are rich, famous, or attractive. Today I would only insert freedom instead of happiness, *à la* Simone de Beauvoir.

My mother is the one who read *The Little Prince* to my brother and me when we were young, and still to this day she reminds us that Antoine de Saint-Exupéry was not an idealist, because people truly are happier if they have flowers on their balconies: he was merely a realist. She is always holding on to the Little Prince motto that what is essential to the heart is invisible to the eye.

It is through my mother's retelling of Kundera's *Slowness* that I could so vividly imagine the cavalier and the woman walking up to the door of the lady's château, both intensely aware that upon their first sight of that door, they have to bid one another farewell. Slowly they reach the door, and at that very moment the lady turns around, uttering the words "I have a complaint to make." Listening to my mother tell her version of Kundera's *Slowness*, I knew there was nothing slower than the lady's method used to actively, but with passive slowness, discover a way to prolong her time with her cavalier.

Yes, that is my mother, and I have to confess that nobody can generate the dilemmas of intimacy in me as she does.

I am often reminded of Arthur Schopenhauer's well-known little story about porcupines when I think of her, a story Freud enjoyed enough to include it in his book on group psychology. The story goes like this:

A troop of porcupines is milling about on a cold winter's day. In order to keep from freezing, the animals move closer together. Just as they are close enough to huddle, however, they start to poke each other with their quills. In order to stop the pain, they spread out, lose the advantage of contact, and begin to shiver. This sends them back in search of each other, and the cycle repeats as they struggle to find a comfortable distance between entanglement and freezing.

Are we not all continuously caught in the porcupines' struggle to reach the optimal distance where one can find the most heat yet be poked by the Other to the least possible extent? Are we all not caught on a cold winter day in a compulsive attempt to find as much warmth as possible in our various relationships, with the fewest possible quills? Of course, each individual's definition of heat and quills varies according to their own narrative. I am merely referring to the struggles of intimacy, the struggle between entanglement and freezing; or maybe, to put it in Lacanian terms, it is not the distance from the Other that produces anxiety, but the overwhelming closeness to the Other that is accompanied by raw anxiety for each one of us.

And, as Freud reminds us, "The evidence ... shows that almost every intimate emotional relation between two people which lasts for some time—marriage, friendship, the relations between parents and children—contains a sediment of feelings of aversion and hostility, which only escapes perception as a result of repression. ..."

I am indeed inclined to define "competent" mothering, paradoxically, as the ability to resist an optimal distance from one's children. I know that it might sound absurd, but I would have to define a "good enough mother" as a mother who loves violently. A mother who cannot resist getting as close as possible, providing all the warmth in the world for the child, but of course simultaneously and inevitably pricking the child with quite a lot of quills. It seems that mothers cannot love any other way, no matter what their intellect tells them, unless they are dead. As such, mothering is inevitably accompanied by violent and claustrophobic loving; mothers need to be aware of that and continually struggle with it. They should all consider themselves part of a group, the group for "mothers who love violently"; they should, like alcoholics and drug addicts, know that their battle with violent love is a lifelong battle, and they should take it one day at a time, knowing they are swimming upstream. Their group greeting would go something like this: "Hi, my name is K, and I am a mother; I have not loved violently for two weeks now," and then the audience should clap, and shout: "Good for you, K!"

Of course there are things that might aid a mother in this ongoing battle, such as having a life of her own, having herself had a mother who had a life of her own, and, above all, creativity. But none of these things is enough to shield the mother-child relationship from the disasters of violent loving; you have to be continually aware of it, never believe you are cured, for it could easily slip out of your control.

For, seriously, can one really come upon a flesh-and-blood mother (not one who is only found in verse) who submits without a fight to her child's desire to separate from her? Can we find a relatively "normal" child who has not suffered the torment of "to separate or not to separate"?

And yet I am in complete agreement with Kristeva when she says:

> In order to think, one must first lose the mother. . . . At that point the self can rediscover the mother, but not as it once knew her. On the contrary, the self never stops re-creating the mother through the very freedom it gained from being separated from her. The mother is a woman who is always renewed in images and in words, through a process of which "I" am the creator simply because I am the one who restores her.

As such, if I may say so, Odysseus and I both made the symbolic move to our motherlands at some level, in an attempt to re-find the warmth we had lost, to re-create our internal mothers; once we felt we had managed to grow thicker skins, and were able to tolerate the quills of closeness.

Today I anticipate Ms. N's arrival for our first session after her vacation; it is five o'clock in the afternoon and I am exhausted, because I have already seen five patients. But why so fatigued? In Boston I was able to see up to eight patients a day at times, and although I would feel tired, never did I experience such a degree of emotional exhaustion. This feeling of being worn out has accompanied me since the first day of my return to Tehran; it is as though here I am trapped in a never-ending cycle of feelings; it is as though my wonderful, well-established, deeply needed defenses have been suddenly taken away from me.

I remember that when, as a little girl in Canada, I was asked why I had immigrated, I would respond in a nostalgic tone of voice: "I was so attached to my homeland that I had to move thousands of miles away." I wonder if this is why many of us stay away for so long, in order not to endure the overwhelming feelings of being back near our olive tree. Staying away somehow functions as a vehicle against the inevitable, loaded emotionality of every single individual's ordinary return.

In Tehran I feel a greater sadness for my students, for people I observe in the street; I have to watch cruel and merciless old age take over my grandparents. It is so much harder to forget about my father's ongoing battle with sleep, manifested in his persistent insomnia. In Tehran I cannot escape the existence of old and struggling relatives, but most of all my homeland has reawakened my severe and punitive superego, in the form of condemning me not only to do what I do not want to do, but to enjoy doing it. In my motherland, the moment I decide to do as I please, I am left with nothing but guilt.

I feel more identified with everything and everybody in Tehran, which leads to a great deal more emotional exhaustion in all scenarios, including with patients. It is also emotionally loaded, for at times I despise the way I identify with people here. I have spent years separating myself from them, because I am not supposed to be who I was when I left. I hate the fact that, in the most ordinary of senses, regardless of who I thought I had become, I identify with what, in the most clichéd terms, are "my people." I find myself identifying and rediscovering parts of myself that I have worked hard at expelling, at getting rid of: parts I did not want to acknowledge, parts which I believed I had slowly gotten rid of over twenty years.

In my homeland I have to tolerate the anxieties of the "return of the repressed," or, as Seneca puts it succinctly:

> One never comes back home with the same moral character one went out with; something or other becomes unsettled where one had achieved internal peace; some one or other of the things one had put to flight reappears on the scene.

I was supposed to have turned into a person who does not make such a split between "Us" and "Them"; I was supposed to have subjectivity, to follow my desires, to be comfortable with various parts of my being, to have my superego under control and to have developed a strong and well-established ego. In short, I had imagined myself to be a much more analyzed person than I turned out to be.

I wonder what it was like for Odysseus. Was he overwhelmed by all that he had to feel? Was he melancholic because the olive tree had become ancient by the time of his return? Was he sad to observe Penelope's wrinkles, at which he probably found himself obsessively looking? Was Odysseus disappointed to recognize what an ordinary man he still was, in spite of his great and extraordinary adventures?

I do not believe that Odysseus' conflict upon his return was due solely to the changes within him, his people's lack of interest in who he had become, or the changes that had occurred in his homeland, though certainly those were significant parts of it.

I have an idea that Odysseus' return, like mine, was full of torment, anguish, and melancholia, for he had to come face to face with how little he had changed, how the greatest adventures of all time had managed to leave several parts of him untouched.

In a sense, and every single day since the day of my return, I am terrified of coming to resemble the most ordinary of characters in my hometown.

I believe Odysseus suffered, paradoxically, both from the great changes that had occurred in him and in his hometown during his time away, but also from the many ways that he and his olive tree *had not changed*, because everything within him and all that surrounded him had remained exactly the way he remembered them. Sometimes what tortures us most upon our return home are the ways in which we, and our home, have remained exactly the way we remember them.

Ms. N enters in a very Parisian mood, recounting her recent visit to Paris in such beautiful and affect-laden language that I feel momentarily that the boundaries between my patient and me have dissolved, and we have rejoined each other in a very pleasurable, narcissistic union.

I have an idea that there is clear reparation happening on Ms. N's part. Now that the separation is over and we are once again reunited, there is no need for stormy seas or knives; we can once again resume our lily-of-the-valley affair. It feels as if we have a very calm sea today, one in which both analytic subjects can indulge.

Ms. N reports: "What saddens me is that if we were having our sessions in Paris, I would have a lot more interesting stuff to tell you. Here it seems I can only tell you about banal, petty, and uninteresting matters, stuff that frustrates me. For example, since I take a taxi to come to your office, every single time I am stunned by the extent of the 'third-worldness' and stupidity of these cab drivers. Sitting behind them, I cannot believe how fast and in what an uncivilized way they drive; it is as if laws are only there to be broken by them. Also they always have their brainless, ugly, and un-sophisticated music turned up so loud, with absolutely no consideration for the passenger; what if I do not want to hear it? Why is it that Iranians have no respect for one's personal space? It is so easy for them to intrude upon one."

(Here I wonder if I have been too intrusive, have not been considerate enough of my passenger. Have I been telling Ms. N things she does not want to hear? Have I been breaking any of the laws of our analytic contract? Have we been going too fast in this analysis?

Or is she unconsciously informing me about her own "third-worldness," warning me of her own unsophistication, brainlessness, and ugliness. Are they parts of herself that she is projecting onto the cab drivers: the parts of herself that she cannot tolerate, the parts she needs to expel?)

Ms. N continues: "Have you seen these couples who get on their motorbikes, with the men in front, of course, and the women behind carrying an infant? None of them is wearing a helmet, no protection for their heads; I get so angry: don't they realize how easy it is for the baby to get hurt? You see, Doctor" (it seems that in the name of reparation I have regained my title), "Here, I can only tell you these ordinary things."

(I can hear in her discourse the information she is trying to reveal to me: she is saying "Doctor, do not be fooled by my sophisticated discourse and strong presence, I am very fragile; my head has no protection; I am an infant on so many different levels, an infant who is terrified of getting injured, who feels in danger, with no protective helmet for her head.")

I ask her: "Are you under the impression that you should only tell me extraordinary things? What is wrong with telling me ordinary things?"

After a brief silence, Ms. N replies: "What is coming to my mind is Proust, you know in his book *In Search of Lost Time*, Swann, the main character, who is very sophisticated, cultured, worldly, and intellectual, absolutely enamored with the aristocratic circle he moves in, falls in love with Odette, who is kind of a cheap prostitute, lacking grace and sophistication. I have always admired Swann's ability to love such a girl, not to be bound by everything that he was himself. He was able to love a girl who was lower than himself; he was able not to be imprisoned by the long list of qualities a girl must have to be worthy of his love. I wish I could be like that."

No matter what the topic, Ms. N's discourse always stays faithful to her psychic dynamic of low versus high, ordinary versus extraordinary, Paris versus Tehran, Swann versus Odette, aristocracy versus commonness, and so on, with one subject always in a higher, more privileged, chic, intellectual, and desirable position than the Other. Suddenly some aspects of my countertransferential feelings become clear to me: from the beginning of my relationship with Ms. N, I have at times anxiously found myself in the position of the unsophisticated Odette; a cheap prostitute in the face of Ms. N's highly sophisticated art and Swann-like features. At other times, however, there would be a reversal of our position: Ms. N would be the one identified with Odette, and I would occupy the space that belonged to the all-powerful, extraordinary analyst who, despite my youth, possessed something that she was paying me to access.

This dynamic of highness versus lowness seems to be at the core of Ms. N's psychic structure. No wonder she is always so preoccupied with saying interesting things and being extraordinary; no wonder I have chosen a lexis of ordinary, extraordinary, greatness, banality, and so on to describe the case of my *ideal patient.*

Indeed it seems, after all, that there is a clear investment on her part in *being* my ideal patient, which she has successfully managed to do: the special patient, the *chosen one* for me to write about. From a Freudian point of view, none of this has been an accident. In my opinion, the process by which an analyst chooses to write about a patient always entails an enactment of the unconscious dynamics of both analytic subjects; the case of Ms. N and me is no exception. It could be said that this extraordinary case adheres to the most ordinary of psychoanalytic rules.

I have an idea that one way of directing the treatment of Ms. N would be to move her away from these forms of all-or-nothing, black-or-white distinctions: for her and for me to both become comfortable tolerating both the Odette and the Swann in us with ambivalence, for indeed, they are both in all of us.

At this point Ms. N reports a dream she had the night before: "I dreamt that I was in bed naked with this man, but I was pretty sure nothing had happened between us; all I could think about was getting out of bed and facing the dirty nightgown on the floor near the bed. I was so disgusted by its dirtiness. I did not want to look at it, to face it, and while I was getting up from the bed to finally do it, I woke up from the dream in a panic."

(I wonder again if the dirtiness of a piece of clothing, a garment that she is trying to face but cannot in the dream, stands for the ugliness, the unsophistication, the brainlessness; basically, all the dirtiness within herself; all that is lacking in her; all that she does not want to look at. In a sense, the process of analysis is waking her, forcing her to look at herself.

This time, as in her previously recurring dream, the dream is not allowing her to leave without this missing article of clothing. It sounds to me as though Ms. N must get up from her metaphoric sleep, open her eyes to all the worst and dirtiest parts of herself (recognize the Odette within her), face all that is missing in her, and finally put the dirty article of clothing on. This, I believe, might lead to a reduction of anxiety: if she were to become able to board the departing ship in her dream and face the chaos and dirtiness within herself. Because when she externalizes the turmoil, ignores it, leaves it behind, she only finds that the Odette in her has followed her, taking the form of severe anxiety and very stormy seas. The act of wearing and accepting these parts of herself, I believe, might lead to the possibility of smooth sailing, instead of turbulent seas and disasters.)

I respond to Ms. N's dream with: "What kind of dirt was on the nightgown?"

Ms. N replies in a very agitated voice: "What do you mean? Dirt is just dirt is just dirt. A good question would have been who the man in bed with me was. You are not very smart sometimes, are you?"

I respond: "I can be very stupid sometimes."

Ms. N starts laughing intensely; she cannot stop, and she says: "I can never admit to my stupidity: you might be stupid, but you are courageous.

"You know, Doctor, before I leave I want to share something with you. I have been wondering why in all my years away from Iran my preferred mode of mental disorder was depression, but since I moved back home, I never feel depressed but often anxious instead. I know our time is up." As Ms. N leaves my office, I find myself thinking of Odysseus yet again. Was he more anxious after his return? Is it the closeness of the Other, the fear of being engulfed by it, that constitutes the nucleus of anxiety (as Lacan tells us), while separation from the object is accompanied by melancholia but not anxiety?

I am not certain if one can make a metatheory from this notion, but what I do know is that I have become familiar with anxiety. I am now much more intimately acquainted with its territory since my return to my motherland. Meanwhile my favorite mode of keeping busy, nostalgia, has left me for the time being. I agree with Kundera yet again: nostalgia is the territory of the motherland.

I often feel anxious in my motherland, for I can easily become engulfed in the inevitable closeness to individuals. While, on the other hand, when I was away from my olive tree there was a safe distance in all my relationships from the first moment of encounter, a distance that my interpersonal relations in Tehran do not easily grant me.

Let me make an attempt at clarification by giving you a very common first-encounter dialog, one you might have with anyone when you live in a place that you are not originally from. This is how it goes:

"Hi, my name is Gohar."

"That is an interesting name; where do you come from?"

"I am from Persia." (Persia always sounds more exotic than Iran; it usually triggers the fantasy of faraway lands immediately.)

"How long have you been here?"

"Do you like it here, or do you miss home?"

"Do you plan to ever go back?"

"Are your parents here?"

"Why did you move here?"

This kind of "regular" first meeting then continues around a theme of what I would call *absence.* The conversation is all about what your name is not; whom you miss; where you did not come from; what you left behind; where your parents were not; when you will leave, and so on: utterly in absence and thus at an inevitable distance; a wonderful lack of intimacy. These conversations provide a way of avoiding an excess of affects; a way out of our natural fears of dependency, attachment, and proximity to the Other; a functional defense against our fears of annihilation by the Other.

Upon our return to the motherland, we feel as though all of these defenses are out of order. We don't have a foreign accent, our dark black hair has become ordinary, and our names no longer arouse curiosity. So we have considerably fewer ways of distancing ourselves from other people, of eluding connections. All that we have left at our disposal is to feel, feel, and feel; this leads to a claustrophobic response.

We fantasize daily, and every minute of the day, and dream each night of packing a simple bag (with no more than a toothbrush, no baggage!) that promises a journey home, safe and sound. Home to a land where we were untouchable, where our exoticism provided a shield against all the anxiety and anguish that comes hand in hand with your closeness to your olive tree.

So you can envision my surprise one day, while chatting with an incredibly wise supervisor who had made the decision to move back to his native city twenty years ago. As we were walking in the streets of his heartbreakingly charming city, he said: "When I moved back home, I, like many others, was encapsulated with an assortment of illusions of what a paradise awaited me. Everyone warned me about the disillusionments that would follow. However, I have to inform you, Gohar, twenty years on I have not regretted for one second that I made the decision to return home. Since the moment of my return I have felt at home, day after day. Day after day I have felt that I am where I am supposed to be; and what else matters?"

Hearing my kind supervisor's voice brought me confusion, pain, and jealousy, but also hope. If it could happen to him, then maybe someday it would happen to me.

A Few Years
after Returning
to Tehran

Now, as I write these words, months have passed since I first started putting my thoughts into writing, and a few years have passed since my return. I have to confess that I am very far from enjoying the kind of psychic health my supervisor displayed. However, there are moments when I feel very close to him and his assertions about the motherland.

Some days I work at a clinic where I am exposed to the various kinds of people of my motherland: people from the villages and the city, rich people and people from very low socioeconomic backgrounds, the old and the very young, men and women who I never had a clue about before. I hear their stories all day long. Slowly I am starting to learn their language, and I feel close to them; I am touched by some of their hearts. I am angry at some of their illusions. I get frustrated by their absolute need to get better fast, treating me the way they treat fortune-tellers. Their demand of me to "Tell me everything is going to be OK; you *will* make me feel better, right, Doctor?"

Yet in the middle of all of this chaos, for which my university books and all the theory in the world could not prepare me, though it may sound clichéd, I love them. I feel compassion and an irresistible sense of devotion. I feel as if I am supposed to be right here with them. I feel that they are teaching me to be a street-smart psychoanalyst: one who can function without her couch and fancy office and elaborate theories; one who might learn how to survive her homeland without falling apart; one who might someday be able to utter the words "I have no regrets about returning home."

This discourse reminds me of a young suicidal male patient I have at the clinic, who shows up dressed all in black, and whose only conscious demand is for me to listen to him and eventually agree that it is his right to kill himself. He elaborates beautifully on the pain of the human condition, on the essence of pain and of solitude, and on all the very legitimate reasons one can have for committing suicide. I ask him one day how come he has not yet killed himself.

He responds: "Have you ever looked at your mother's face when she has prepared your favorite meal? Have you ever bitten into a just-ripe peach in the middle of a summer day? Have you ever decided to spend a few thousand *toman*" (the equivalent of two dollars) "on a meal, even though you are so stingy that it goes against every grain in your body? Those are the moments that keep me alive. The truth is, I have not yet decided if I want to be so revengeful."

A young girl of twenty-four walks into my office, covered from head to toe in a very thick black chador which exposes only her big brown eyes. She sits down and starts crying as soon as I utter the words "What brings you here?"

She replies: "What brings me here? What brings me here? I have lost the one thing no woman should ever lose." And then she sits there, crying hysterically and looking at me, waiting for a response.

I find myself dumbfounded. I am trying as hard as I can to think of what it might be: what has she lost? Absolutely unable to come up with the answer, I ask her to elaborate. She looks at me and whispers: "You really do not know; I have heard that you people can be bizarre. But how can a woman not intuitively know what I am referring to? I have lost my virginity, and because of it I had to move out of my parents' house. Not because they asked me to, but I just had to. I do not deserve to eat their bread and butter anymore; I am a disgrace; I do not deserve their kindness anymore; I have dishonored my father's name. I should not pollute their sacred home."

A very big, macho truck-driver comes in, saying: "I heard there is a psychoanalyst in this clinic, and I want to understand myself better." I am ashamed of how I feel, because I have to face what by now, it has become painfully clear, are my own value judgments, since I expected any response from him except a desire for self-knowledge. But why should this be so? Can't big, macho truck-drivers desire to know themselves? Later on, I learn that he is afraid of the dark, and has made his wife leave the lights in their bedroom on every night for the last twelve years.

I will never forget the day he came in and told me: "Doctor, I had a dream I was having sex with my mother the other night. This unconscious is messing with my honor; you have got to heal my soul; I am at your mercy. When I awoke from my dream I started talking to my unconscious, begging it to stop producing these horrifying images. I could not tell you before, but a few nights earlier I had another dream that I was having sex with both my sister and my sister-in-law at the same time."

F, a young girl who moved to Tehran from Isfahan to study journalism just a few years back, comes to see me. Comfortably throwing herself onto the big leather chair in my office, she crosses her legs and says: "I am here to talk to you about my sexuality. I enjoy having sex, but only if I am not in a passive position: I like to initiate sex. I do not like boundaries when it comes to sexual pleasure. I am not shy; I like to be on top sometimes, and I definitely have to have an orgasm." I ask her what she thinks the problem is.

She says: "Iranian men do not like that. I have just had to dump a boyfriend again because he kept asking me to be passive, telling me that he could not perform if I initiated sex. The words that turned him on were 'no' or 'stop,' while what turns me on are 'yes' and 'don't stop.' He told me: 'You will never find a husband with your overt sexual behavior. A woman should always hide the fact that she is enjoying sex. Only prostitutes are supposed to get pleasure out of sex, not decent women.' This is my problem, Doctor. I need you to help me find a man who lets me be the person I really am during sex: a woman who very much enjoys having sex."

A very intellectual thirty-two-year-old man brings me his conflict about having fallen deeply in love with a married woman. He tells me in his first session: "I love her and she loves me too, and yet something does not allow her to let me make love to her. We've been together for almost a year now, and every month I have been allowed to conquer a new territory of her body. First we held hands, then I kissed her, and then slowly she allowed me to touch other parts. The most amazing part of this whole endeavor is that what she allows me to conquer she can never take back from me. That area becomes mine. The next time I am allowed to go at least that far. Even if she does not feel like it, she feels obligated to let me go where I have already gone. What she gives me she can never take back. It is like climbing a mountain: every time one attains a new height, one can put one's flag there. Her small, delicate body is full of my flags now."

A rich, attractive, forty-four-year-old architect shows up for our initial session impeccably dressed. She has a very delicate white blouse on, which covers only one shoulder and leaves her other shoulder bare and exposed. She says: "Oh, how I wish you had the famous picture Freud had above his couch; you know, he took the picture to London with him. I read somewhere that it is a portrait of hysteria. It shows a bare-shouldered woman, in a trance or something like that, fainting into the strong arms of her doctor during a medical demonstration. And rows of interested doctors are watching her. It is so dazzling.

"I was so intrigued by this image when I saw it up close and personal in London that I felt obliged to do some research on it. It is Brouillet's *Une leçon clinique à la Salpêtrière*" (she says it with a perfect French accent). "The patient is Blanche Wittman; she was referred to as the Queen of the Hysterics. The man catching her is Joseph Babinski, and the seated physician orchestrating the whole demonstration is the famous Jean-Martin Charcot.

"You know that the image of hysteria looms over Freud's couch. Well, now I am here because I, like Blanche, keep fainting, and it is becoming both hazardous and embarrassing. Being an architect, I have to be on building sites, and I keep fainting in front of all my male workers. The other day, if one of them had not been strong and observant enough to catch me right away, I would have fallen from a seven-story building and died. Oh, it was so embarrassing. You have to help me with my fainting."

K, a forty-year-old woman who walked into my office about a year ago, has just gone through chemotherapy due to breast cancer, and had one breast removed. She has lost all her hair, and her eyebrows, yet one can still observe the remains of a striking woman, who even in her current dire state has a certain attractiveness about her.

She specifically wanted psychoanalysis, as she informed me during our initial session: "I need help with my sex drive. I heard Freud used such a term, and I have been on a sexual mission ever since I can remember. I need help. I have tried many other forms of treatment, and while they can be helpful, I feel they have failed at really solving my problem. I feel I have a very analyzable character."

After a few more sessions we agree to a four-times-a-week analysis. In her first session, she tells me that I should not be fooled by her avant-garde discourse and appearance, for she actually comes from a very traditional family environment, with an extremely strict, emotionally unavailable father, and a mother who had the function of a sacrificial lamb within the family. Her rebelliousness, artistic ambitions, and crazy lifestyle have always been looked upon by her family with suspicion, and her father has on many occasions referred to her as a whore.

K elaborates in the first few sessions on how angry she has always found herself at her mother for being so weak, for not having a life of her own, for being, as she puts it, under her father's whip. Her relationship with her father was ambivalent: while she took him to be the symbol of manhood and what a real man should be like, K also found herself rebelling against his ideal of how a good Muslim woman should behave. She also took all her complaints about her mother to him, and he would always take K's side, and jokingly say: "In the end you will manage to get me to divorce your mother, so you and I can be together." As K recalls this statement, she reports having a sensation of complete ecstasy.

There was a very seductive authenticity and courage to her discourse. She was never boring; she was always full of affect. I found her extremely entertaining, and, as time went by, I was not surprised to find out that she was in the entertainment business.

The initial problem K presented when she started analysis was that she was involved with A, a very rich, unattractive (the word she actually used to describe his appearance was "deformed"), and sadistic man, who lied to her and cheated on her continually, and was only capable of having extremely humiliating and degrading sexual relations with her.

They met regularly three to four times a week, from about eight to ten o'clock in the evening. As soon as she walked into his apartment, he would throw her on the dining table and perform anal intercourse on her from behind, with most of her clothes still on, and in her words: "He never even offers me a glass of water, nor is he ever considerate of the fact that I suffer from physical pain due to chemotherapy. After we've had sex for a few hours, he will not hold me, or want to have dinner with me. I never even shower there; he just drives me home. Instead he always buys me something incredibly expensive the day after; anything from a car to covering all my medical expenses, trips to Europe, expensive clothes. And he also gives me a lot of cash on a continuing basis." These episodes are followed not only with monetary gain but with guilt, shame, and severe anxiety for K.

K shows up to her morning session on the day after such nights in a very devastated state of being, reporting: "I feel like such a whore. In a way I don't know what difference there is between me and a whore. I guess it is like the Kiarostami movie where the whore tells the woman who is married to a rich guy that the only difference between them is that *she* is a wholesaler. I am sleeping with him for money; I only started dating him because he was so rich. I guess I must be a high-class whore; you know I have slept with many men during my life, and never have I achieved orgasm. I hate how humiliated I feel when he takes me home just after having fucked me. Sometimes I am so overwhelmed with raw anxiety that my mouth becomes full of blood from clenching my teeth so madly.

"Yet I must be honest with you: I never get turned on by gentle, loving men, men who make love to a woman, good-looking men. I complain about what A does not give me, but there is a part of me that only gets sexually aroused if I am in a humiliating position. It is as if somehow I am attracted to dirt and ugliness. A is so disgusting, with his fat belly and bald head; his left hand is totally deformed and he is sixteen years older than me. I wonder why I am not turned on by men my own age, with flat bellies and attractive figures, men who are gentle lovers."

This discourse has led, I believe, to some very important associations for K, since she continues: "I am reminded of how I lost my virginity. I was sixteen years old and dating my first husband, who was a couple of years older than me; a very ill, almost schizophrenic drug addict. One night we were in the middle of nowhere in his car, it was very dark, there was nobody else about, it was a very filthy road and there was lots of garbage and dirt around us. We started having sex, and for the rest of my life I never forgot the sudden appearance of a few wild dogs and their barking around our car while I was losing my virginity in the middle of nowhere to a loser, who would end up being the father of my children and my first husband."

The other association following this scene was the way her father has always clearly communicated to her that her choice of profession, her behavior, her way of dressing, and her artistic endeavors were all for whores.

One can imagine a sadistic paternal scene, symbolized by the men she chooses, by what turns her on in them, and she is unable to perceive a man as a man if he is not, in a sense, sadistic.

One day, after eight months of analysis, having broken up with A, she comes in and starts talking about E. E is the new man she has just met. She finds him very different from A and the rest of the men she has been in relationships with, including both of her previous husbands. This man is sophisticated and attractive; he is an art dealer who speaks various languages and comes from an aristocratic background.

K informs me of the disgust she felt for this man as soon as she walked into his perfectly decorated house, with various French cheeses on the table, and wine served the way it would be in a château in France. "Please, what kind of a real man is so much into beauty and sophistication? He has to be gay.

"You know, everything around him is already too beautiful; there is no space for me to do anything. It is through lots of anxiety, drama, continuous action and ups and downs that I feel I exist. Ease is not my mode of obtaining pleasure. I have to find a masculine man" (sadistic) "and then take it away from him" (castration, penis envy). "I feel more alive in a humiliating sexual position than anywhere else in my life. Maybe that is why I like to have lots of bad sex."

With K I always have the feeling that she is an overexcited child; excitement seems to be the equivalent of being alive for her. If she is not in a continuous state of doing, she feels dead. As she says one day: "I would much rather be manic than depressed, depression is accompanied by death and darkness; mania is how I choose to live my life. That is how I feel alive."

While seeing patients like the ones mentioned above every day since my return to Tehran, I cannot help but think of André Green's paper: "Has Sexuality Anything to Do with Psychoanalysis?"

Just by running a simple Google search one quickly becomes aware that Green is not the only one raising such concerns and proposing such debates. Contemporary psychoanalysis seems to be full of questions such as "Where have all the hysterics gone?," "Do we still have neurotic patients on our couches?," "Yesterday's hysterics are today's borderlines," "Neurosis: a myth of the past," and "Does anybody talk about sex anymore in psychoanalysis?"

Observing the psychoanalytic literature, one can only confirm Green's position: that the fashionable "in" themes dominating most of the analytic literature in recent years have definitely been narcissistic disorders, borderline disorders, bipolarity, and psychotic states. Meanwhile, analysts seem to be more interested in hearing issues that are predominantly about aggression and its vicissitudes as opposed to sexuality in their patients' discourses. The pages of our journals are full of pre-Oedipal psychoanalytic theories, leaving one with a nostalgic feeling for the era of Oedipus the king.

There have been various explanations for this shift, ranging from Kristeva's assertion that it is a paradoxical attempt to exclude the mother from language, to whether the patterns of psychopathology are changing (patients). Or is it our diagnostic categories that have changed (analysts)? Or is this change the result of multiple sociocultural dynamics? And so on, and so on.

My clinical observations—for example, the ones reported here—seem to answer Green's question: I have found sexuality in Tehran. In Tehran, today's sexuality is still Freud's sexuality. Since the very beginning my couch has been full of good old hysterics, and various other kinds of neurotic. In short, in Tehran I have encountered a kind of patient who is very much in line with the kinds of patients Freud was seeing during his time, a kind of patient that reminds me of a time when psychoanalysis was still in its early years.

I have also been astonished at the candor and willingness of patients in expressing sexual material openly within the sessions. Especially considering the traditional Iranian cultural base, where sexuality is supposed to be a lot more repressed and taboo than within Western cultures.

But let us go on:

Another young female patient, recently divorced, comes into her first session saying that she wants to be analyzed because she is *haunted by memories and regrets*. I have always thought of her as Gradiva, Jensen and Freud's Gradiva, and she reports upon arrival: "I remember observing my wedding band, staring at it, trying to comprehend what had happened. How come my left hand looked like somebody else's hand? I had married the man I loved, I could not imagine marrying anyone else, and yet my wedding band, the one I had picked out with the utmost care and attention, the one on which my mother-in-law had had both our names engraved, a wedding band that encapsulated my very personal touch—on my finger it made me feel as if I was living somebody else's life, a life which I was observing from a distance. As if I was outside of it and everything was happening to a character in a film, one who looked like me but was not me.

"Today I took my wedding band off for the first time since my wedding day, almost six years ago. Never once had I taken it off before. And now I stare at my left hand the same way I did as a newlywed, and I find my bare hand once again unfamiliar without my delicate band. What has stayed constant is that my divorce, like my marriage, is happening to someone else. I am still watching it happen, as if to a character in a movie."

As my patient is talking, I am elaborating in my head:

Do we distance ourselves from our immediate experiences, especially emotionally loaded ones such as marriage and divorce, in order not to have to face our own participation in everything that happens to us? Do we resist the intensity of our emotions by distancing ourselves from the immediacy of our experiences?

At this point she lies down on my couch of her own accord, putting herself into a fetal position, and she continues in a much softer voice:

"Divorce, divorrrrce, divorceeee, d-d-d-divorce . . . I find myself pronouncing it in many different ways. It is as if I have the mission of normalizing it by uttering the word in an obsessive manner.

"During my marriage I used to use the word 'divorce' as a mode of getting attention, as a very unsuccessful method of seduction. In a way it was a very aggressive way of threatening my husband, whose body would go very tense, his eyes turning totally emotionless every time I uttered the D-word. And yet for me, at the time, that word was like any other word; I could use it easily, and my communication was like that of the most ordinary woman. I am desperate. Please love me more.

"So how come that today, after my divorce, the word has become so significant to me? I can never use it without feeling like I am going to choke on it, like my whole body aches; the word divorce has assumed horrible colors and God-awful smells.

"I am not quite certain of the reasons behind such a drastic change. All I can convey is my personal experience, without claiming any truth to it.

"Is it because the word has now become impregnated with my personal experiences of the last few months, with my mother's pale, terrified face when my divorce was announced to her, her sense of guilt over what she might have done wrong, what she could have done differently, and the anxiety of an uncertain future for her daughter? And, above all, there is not enough distance between us for her to be an observer of what is going on; she is there, in the middle of it all, everything that is happening to me feels like it were happening to her too.

"How can I ever utter the word divorce without being haunted by the image of my maternal grandfather, who, acting like a 1920s chevalier, without informing any of us, his slender, tall figure walking into my husband's office, unannounced, just to leave a note, a note containing a poem, followed by 'Call me, please.' My grandfather has been settling disputes all his life, disputes which no one could believe he had the courage, compassion, and authentic sense of democracy to smoothly overcome. Surely he had thought to himself: 'I can find a way to rescue my granddaughter's marriage.'

A Few Years after Returning to Tehran

"How can I ever use the word divorce, without reliving the terrifying images of what was reported to me from the meeting between my husband and my grandfather?

"I can visualize it clearly, as if I was present. I can imagine my husband with dark circles under his eyes, his hands trembling with shame, unable to stop his leg from shaking, and absolutely unaware of how he has reached this point. It's just like my estranged hands: he must feel that this must surely be happening to somebody else. He finds the encounter the most humiliating and shameful he has ever had to endure in his whole life.

"I can see him walking in, covered in sweat, unable to look my grandfather in the eye. He attempts to kiss his hand; my grandfather does not allow him to; he cares about him too much, like a son, a son he has never before seen in such a painful and formal setting. My husband kisses his shoulder instead, while they both sit down. My grandfather tries to say everything he can gather the strength to say. I can hear his voice breaking up, he gets like that under extreme emotional situations, he can hardly breathe; finally he says: 'Could you two please reconsider?'

"My husband has tears in his eyes; his heart is shredded to pieces; he would rather lose everything that has been dear to him than disobey this respectable elderly man's wishes—a man he has gotten to know over the years, a man for whom he has the utmost respect. Suddenly, out of all the memories he shares with my grandfather, perhaps as an attempt to lighten the situation inside his head, he remembers bringing him his favorite kind of brown sugar cubes.

"My husband is brought back to the stifling room where one cannot ignore the heaviness and the intensity. He feels hot; he feels as if he is going to pass out; he is absolutely overwhelmed by what he is bound to say; he has no choice but to disobey my grandfather. It is just completely out of his hands. It is as if he just does not have the psychic tools to reverse the situation. By now he is feeling like Saddam when the Americans were taking over Iraq, when he knew he did not have a chance, yet he could not back down. But he does not have the heart to hurt my grandfather either. He is torn between what his head and his heart are telling him. He knows in his head that he has made the right decision; he has thought about it; there are certain things he knows about which have happened and can never now be reversed. And yet his heart is absolutely incapable of disobeying this respectable man's request—this man, he realizes at this very moment, whom he has come to love and will intensely miss.

"Above all, the most painful realization for him is that he will walk out of this meeting a very different man to the one who arrived; he knows he will never be the same man after today, and that knowledge will continue to drive him into nothingness and anguish.

"How will I ever be able to eradicate my father's sense of helplessness, his sheer vulnerability, from my mind? It has been engraved there since the day he walked into my apartment with, of course, his humidifier, his small radio, and a few books. He has dropped everything at his work in another city to rescue his daughter in the middle of her divorce.

"My father walks into my apartment; it must feel strange to him that everything looks exactly as before. I still have the wedding pictures up. It is as if all of the very serious conversations my husband and I had about the inevitableness of our divorce could easily evaporate into thin air, but I was convinced that taking down wedding pictures would be no different from signing divorce papers.

"My father looks tired; he tells me: 'I never wanted you to get married in the first place. I wanted you to pursue your career in philosophy, and there is a part of me that is pleased about your divorce. Staying married and staying in Iran would have ended for you with social gatherings, family parties, the duties of a wife, and ever less and less philosophy. And yet, my heart is broken at the prospect of your divorce; it is as if my heart is aching while my mind has become liberated in celebration of your freedom.'

"Doctor, the strangest sensations came over me while my father was talking. I knew very well that regardless of all the surface façade my husband and I had come up with, I was absolutely the one who had orchestrated this divorce. I had behaved in a manner which, I knew, would leave us nowhere else to go but the divorce courts. At that very moment, while my father was making me fresh orange juice with the radio blasting out, I knew very well that I was getting a divorce in the name of philosophy.

"I felt pathetic; had I really given up the man I loved for philosophy? Was I to spend my many lonely nights contemplating Nietzsche, desperate to understand Heidegger, and in a state of total vertigo over Foucault?

A Few Years after Returning to Tehran

"You are probably going to think that I am crazy, but at that very moment I became overwhelmed with maternal feelings. I really wanted to be pregnant and have a child, to have a traditional life. I was so angry at all these big philosophers; I felt betrayed by them. When I fell in love with philosophy as a little girl, it was supposed to improve my life and make me happy; not lead me here, alone with my books.

"My father said: 'My beautiful girl, philosophy, and especially literature, will rescue you, not I nor your husband nor anyone else. You will see at the end of the day what people like us are equipped with: the gift of a thirst for knowledge, the gift of deriving pleasure from reading, of being a kind of intellectual; this is the best weapon against the banality of life that humanity has ever discovered. You will see, you will see; never give it up, I beg of you.'

"How will I ever be able not to have my heart contract with pain when now I understand what divorce means: one day you are looking for a wedding dress, you are buying glasses and bedlinen for your home, and choosing paintings for your walls, and then . . . The notion of the significance of objects has become clearer to me now . . . It is as Salman Akhtar tells us: immigrants in a new country try very hard to surround themselves with things from their home country: with carpets, paintings and plates and . . . We often hear them talking not so much about the people they miss in their native land as about the streets, the color of the phone booths, the smell of the stores.

"Of course, this nostalgia is not really caused by the smell of the store that an elderly Italian immigrant remembers, but rather by the fact that the smell of the store brings with it the memory of his mother and how he found her the most attractive woman on earth when, on that hot summer afternoon, she was cutting thin slices of prosciutto in that particular store with that particular smell.

"For me, one of the thorniest parts of my divorce has been dealing with the memories induced in me by the various objects left from a life made together.

"I cannot get away from the memory of how we picked a particular picture in Mexico City for our apartment. We did not even have the apartment then, but both of us, in our own ways, started fantasizing about where we would put it, what frame we would buy for it, and who we would like to show it off to. It felt as if we were two young kids playing house.

"Looking at the picture today (which we never did end up framing, it just sat there in a box), I cannot help but reminisce about the specificities of that day. Just looking at the picture brings an endless flow of memories with it, which force themselves upon me, coming from nowhere; little details that I thought had escaped me over the years.

"The day we bought the picture in Mexico City we had fish for lunch at a small local restaurant near the water. I remember how the wind touched my skin as my husband and I sat there in that little restaurant, eating our fish without any notion of time or place; we were eating fish together and we had no other concerns.

"I asked him for the thousandth time: 'How do you know you love me?' Besides philosophy, this might be another reason that we got a divorce: I was never able to stop asking him if he loved me and how much he loved me, and did he love me less than a day ago; did he love me as much as on our wedding day? Insatiably, I kept asking him for confirmation of his love.

"He said: 'Because I do not remember a time when I did not love you, it is as if loving you has obscured the notion of time for me. It is actually quite strange, but now when I remember a childhood memory you are in it. I do not know how to explain it, but you know what I mean. I do not possess any memories that I have not juxtaposed you with.'

"I was not sure exactly what he meant; I did have memories that did not include him, I just found them utterly boring."

A few years after I started working with Gradiva, she married a man who is totally different from her ex-husband. She comes in one day and says: "Driving here, I was pondering about this study that was done in the 1970s in America. I am not sure about the details, but it was a longitudinal study measuring the mental health of kids from very traditional families versus more open-minded, intellectual ones.

"The conservative children of group A had parents who did not talk to them at the kitchen table, where things were not discussed but demanded. Within their families there was a clear-cut distinction between good and evil, and they were told that they were righteous, hard-working, model human beings. On the other hand, their parents reminded them on a daily basis of the losers, and of the menaces in other parts of society, from which they should always differentiate themselves.

A Few Years after Returning to Tehran

"Into their young adulthood the children from group A had steady jobs, lived stable lives with a wife, 2.5 kids and a dog, and looked like they were living the American dream.

"Now, what about the children from group B families? Well, they contemplated philosophy; their lives were chaotic; they were ambivalent human beings. These children had grown into adults who were beyond good and evil; for them the human condition as such was comprised of various shades of gray. They had grown up discussing things at length around their kitchen tables, with parents who were not sure of things, who wanted to hear their opinions and were willing to change their minds at all times. Group B was also where all sorts of creativity were observed.

"Well, when our groups entered adulthood, group A were the biggest consumers of porn, of psychiatric medication; had all sorts of weird tics and obsessions; were guilt-ridden, stiff, in a sense impenetrable. There was also an absolute absence of any creativity.

"Meanwhile group B, if we use your Freudian terms, were suffering from common unhappiness, as opposed to group A's neurotic misery. They were happier, freer, and every single one of them chose to discuss things at length at the kitchen table with their own kids.

A Few Years after Returning to Tehran

"You know, Doctor, I am a child of group B, while my ex-husband was a child of group A, and you cannot take a member of group B into the home of someone from group A without triggering insanity. I always felt like throwing up, felt like shouting 'Things are not black or white, there is always gray, and it is in the gray that we have the best of what our human condition has to offer: like what you and I have been able to produce here!' I was always constructing and reconstructing my stories, allowing for creativity to surface and enabling freedom, as much as is humanly possible.

"However, you know, it was very seductive to join group A through marriage, as though for a while I had found the solution to all the anxieties that accompanied me throughout the days of my uncertain, chaotic, 'everything is relative' lifestyle. I had finally met a hero, one who was convinced he had all the answers, and for a while it felt like ecstasy.

"Do you remember the day you told me that my divorce was my doing, that I had found a way out, that it was my life drive that protected me in that way; otherwise I would have gotten cancer—yes, I forgot to tell you that there were a lot of somatic illnesses in group A. After my divorce I came back to the wonderful chaos of group B, where we lead a postmodern life, talk everything out to the point of nausea, and yet we do not feel like throwing up. Thank you for guiding me home. And you know why you could do it? I am convinced that you talk to your kids at your kitchen table."

My patient's last statement brought this association to my mind; in 1905 Freud wrote:

> "Auntie, speak to me! I'm frightened because it is so dark."
>
> His aunt answered him: "What good would that do? You can't see me."
>
> "That does not matter," replied the child. "If anyone speaks, it gets light."

Just as we are told that the patient says everything in the first session, and it is the analyst who needs time to hear it, I needed the above pages to free-associate on what it meant, for me, to do psychoanalysis in Tehran.

It seems to me that it has been about learning how to love. Lacan used to say: "To love is to give what you haven't got." Which, in the words of Jacques-Alain Miller, means: to love is to recognize your lack and to give it to the Other, to place it in the Other. It's not giving what you possess, like gifts and presents; it's giving something else that you don't possess, which goes beyond you. To do that you have to assume your lack—your "castration," as Freud used to say.

Doing Psychoanalysis in Tehran has been a lover's discourse. I have been taught by every single patient, supervisee, student, etc., "to give what I haven't got."

Understanding that leaves me without any more words to speak to you about doing psychoanalysis in Tehran. For now . . .

It seems that our time is up for this analytic hour.